EZBONI MONDIRI GWONZA

The South Sudanese Nationalist and Politician

by Peter Obadayo Tingwa

A note to readers from the author: Strictly speaking, memoirs may point to some historical facts, but they are not history books.

The publisher wishes to acknowledge and thank Dr. Douglas H. Johnson for his invaluable help and support for Africa World Books and its mission of preserving and promoting African cultural and literary traditions and history. Dr. Johnson and fellow historians have been instrumental in ensuring that African people remain connected to their past and their identity. Africa World Books is proud to carry on this mission.

Copyright © 2023 Peter Obadayo Tingwa

All rights reserved. It is illegal to reproduce, duplicate or transmit any part of this book in either electronic means or printed format. Recording of this publication is strictly prohibited. No part of this publication may be reproduced, stored in a retrieval system, or transmitted, in any form, or by any means, electronic, mechanical, photocopying, recording or otherwise, without the prior permission of the publishers.

ISBN: 9780645972320

This book is sold subject to the conditions that it shall not, by way of trade or otherwise, be lent, re-sold, hired out or otherwise circulated without the publisher's prior consent in any form of binding or cover other than in which it is published and without a similar condition including the condition being imposed on the subsequent purchaser.

Cover design, typesetting and layout: Africa World Books
Unit 3, 57 Frobisher St, Osborne Park, WA 6017
P.O. Box 1106 Osborne Park, WA 6916

DEDICATION

This book is dedicated to my family and to all those South Sudanese who laid the foundation for the struggle which has made South Sudan to be a free independent country today.

CONTENTS

Dedication iii
Acknowledgments ix
Acronyms xi
Foreword xiii

I: Introductory Background 1
II: The Formative Years 9
III: Taking The Plunge Into Politics 27
IV: Political Developments While Ezboni Was In Jail 45
V: Release From Jail, Fall Of Abboud and Back To Politics 54
VI: In The Southern Resistance Movement 69
VII: Ezboni Arrives Home, Challenges and Exploits 80
VIII: In The Government of Azania Liberation Front (ALF) 105
IX: Coup And The End of ALF Government 131
X: Analysis and Reasons for the Coup 142
XI: The Movement After the Collapse of The ALF 158

XII: The Southern Sudan Provisional Government (SSPG)	165
XIII: The Dawning and Realization of the Peace Agreement	171
XIV: In the Southern Sudan Regional Government (SSRG)	180
XV: The Looming Threat to the SSRG and the Adiss Ababa Agreement	188
XVI: The Closing Years	204
XVII: Ezboni, The Man, Politician and Nationalist	209
Appendix I: Approximate Manifesto of the Federal Party	223
Appendix II: New Horizon Issue	225
Bibliography	*229*
Index	*231*

Maps:

Map I: Provinces of the Anglo-Egyptian Sudan	xix
Map II: Amadi (Mundri) District	xx

Plates:

I. Ezboni Mondiri Gwonza Seyi	11
II. Ezboni's Wife. Elizabeth Tombiŋwa Abarayama	12
III. Contemporaries of Ezboni in the Struggle	28
IV. Morris Ägyili Kayanga Ori Lo'dio	31
V: Severino Fuli	114
VI: Brigadier Paul Ali Ghatala	122

VII: Emperor Haile Selassie holds hands
of Ezboni and Abel Alier   176
VIII: The first cabinet of the high executive council
of the Southern Regional Government   178
IX: HEC President Abel Alier cutting the ribbon to open the
Juba Bridge   182

ACKNOWLEDGMENTS

This book could not have been written without valuable inputs, comments and corrections from very many people. At the fore front is Ezboni himself, from whom most personal stories about him were gathered during ordinary conversations over many years. Secondly, I am grateful to my sister Alice Tingwa for her account of the arrest, escape and re-arrest of Ezboni soon after he won the parliamentary elections of 1958. Thirdly, I am grateful to Morris Ägyili who, for many years, was a very close associate and confidant of Ezboni. Morris provided many of the stories about Ezboni in political life. Fourthly, I am also indebted to Lt. Maj. General Scopas Juma Kamonde who provided first-hand information about the Moru Anyanya and especially about the coup against Ezboni Mondiri, the then Secretary of Defence of Joseph Oduho's Azania Liberation Front government. In addition to interviews with them, both Morris and Scopas provided me with hand written articles about what they observed first hand as well as experienced in the Moru Anyanya. In fact, whenever necessary, I have quoted verbatim from their articles; and for this, I am extremely grateful to them. I am also grateful to

John Russie, especially for clarifications, regarding the Anyanya in Kedi'ba under Jackson Garaŋwa (aka Jeke Garaŋwa, as he was popularly) known. As will be seen, Ezboni's differences with Jackson Garaŋwa and the Anyanya unit in Kedi'ba had a significant impact on Ezboni's political standing locally. As mentioned elsewhere, due to reasons beyond my control, I have been unable to get firsthand information from Jackson Garaŋwa and Repent Sunday, who could have provided the other side to some of the stories. This is very much regretted since their input would have corroborated and enriched the story.

Additionally, I have quoted extensively from Severino Fuli's book: *Shaping a free Southern Sudan* as well as from Professor Storrs McCall's then unpublished manuscript and now printed into a book, *The Genesis and Struggle of the Anyanya in Southern Sudan*, written together with Dr. Lam Akol. This book provides one of the best insights into the Anyanya Movement

I am most grateful to Dr. David Bassiouni for the excellent Foreword and his contribution in Chapter XV in which he brought forth the person and leadership qualities of Ezboni Mondiri, even much more than can be found in the main text of the book. Lastly, I am very much indebted to all those who have read the drafts of the book and made corrections and added inputs to the book. Among those are Dr. David Bassiouni, Hon. Kosti Mänibe, Dr. Charles Bakhiet and Dr. Cirino Hiteng. I thank them for their corrections and valuable comments.

While I sincerely thank all those who provided information to me, I take the responsibility for any slips or errors.

- **Prof Peter Tingwa**
Nairobi Kenya August 2023

ACRONYMS

ALF: Azania Liberation Front
(initially ALM, Azania Liberation Movement)
ANAF: Anyanya National Armed Forces
CMS: Church Missionary Society
CPA: Comprehensive Peace Agreement
DUP: Democratic Unionist Party
GHQ: General Headquarters
HEC: High Executive Council
NAS: National Salvation Army
NCO: Non Commissioned Officer
NPG: Nile Provisional Government
NUP: National Unionist Party
PDP: Peoples Democratic Party
PM: Prime Minster
SAC: Sudan Administrative Conference
SACDNU: Sudan African Closed District National Union
(precursor to SANU)
SALF: Sudan African Liberation Front

SANU: Sudan African National Union
SPLM/A: Sudan Peoples' Liberation Movement/Army
SSLM: Southern Sudan Liberation Movement
SSPG: Southern Sudan Provisional Government
SSRG: Southern Sudan Regional Government
SSU: Sudan Socialist Union
SSWA: Southern Sudan Welfare Association

FOREWORD

As the case was, almost all the black African countries freed themselves from the yoke of a single imperialistic and colonial ruler. Not so for the newly independent country of South Sudan. For South Sudan, it was a double yoke that compelled them to first, freeing themselves from the British dominated condominium rule and later from fellow compatriots of the Arabized and Islamized Northern Sudanese. That struggle for freedom took both peaceful (political) and violent (military) forms in which several of their leaders sacrificed and paid the ultimate price for the long struggle of the people of South Sudanese in exercising their inalienable right to self-determination and eventually independence . And the struggle was such that each passing generation built upon the efforts of the predecessors, until independence was achieved in 1911.

Apart from the earlier tribal leaders who resisted the various foreign invaders, the first generation of those individuals who were the Southern Pioneering Leaders in modern politics included the likes of Buth Diu, Benjamin Lwoki, Paul Logali,

Stanislaus Paysama, Daniel Jumi, Eliya Kuze and Abdel Rahman Sule and many others, The second generation, who were better educated and who took over after the August 1955 Uprising, included political giants like of Aggrey Jaden, Marko Rume, Luigi Adwok, Gordon Mourtat, Ezboni Mondiri, Fr. Saturnino Ohure, Joseph Oduho, Abel Alier, William Deng, Joseph Lagu, Hilary Logali and many more. This group was complemented by their military counterparts like Paul Ali Gbatala, Emidio Taffeng Lodongi who led the Torit Mutiny. The last group is the SPLM/A generation which finally threw away the yoke of domination in 1911.

As has been the case, many citations have been made by official sources as well as by the sons and daughters of South Sudan about those leaders who have made outstanding contributions in the struggle for independence. But often, most of those citations, articles and/or books have omitted the name of Ezboni Mondiri Gwonza Seyi, who in my view was one of the political giants that dominated the era from 1954 to 1985, which marked the formative years of the Southern Resistance Movement. Fortunately, this shortfall has now been addressed timely, by Professor Peter Tingwa in this book titled *"Ezboni Mondiri Gwonza Seyi, A Southern Sudanese Nationalist and Politician"*. In reading the book, my confidence is further reaffirmed that Professor Peter Tingwa, whom I know closely from early school days, has brought forth in a powerful and gripping style, the character, exploits, sacrifices, tribulations, successes, failures and nationalism of Ezboni throughout his struggle for the freedom of the people of the then Southern Sudan, for the public to know, feel and grasp.

In my view, Professor Peter Tingwa, more than anyone

else, is exceptionally qualified to write on and about Ezboni for several reasons, firstly, as a member of the same family clan and a close relative, he had the opportunity and advantage to sit, hear and learn firsthand from Ezboni himself. Secondly, he had the chance to obtain information about the exploits, tribulations and achievements of Ezboni directly from his long term and closest confidant Morris Ägyili Kayanga, with whom he was jailed in 1959. Thirdly, though basically a science academician, Peter has over the years educated himself and has become quite conversant with the history and politics of erstwhile Sudan, and particularly of South(ern) Sudan. For example, under the title '*Lest We Forget*) he has written several articles on those events such as the Azande (Nzara) Riots of 25 July1955, the August 1955 Uprising; the Student Sunday Strike of December/January 1960 *et cetera*. Those have served to enlighten the younger generation and have been quoted widely by scholars. Added to these, is his book in Moru Language on the history of Sudan and South Sudan from 2,300 BC to 2009 AD *(*Àmba *Sudan Ro Ndi South Sudan Be)*

The book presents Ezboni as a consummate politician and a South Sudanese nationalist, outlining his role, tribulations and vicissitudes through the phases and episodes of the South Sudanese political development and struggle. It begins by describing his family background, formative years in schools and the university, which all served to influence and shape his political convictions as well as his passion for and lasting legacy of federation for Southern Sudan. These, together with the need to ensure that federalism is included in the permanent constitution for the Sudan that was to be written by the 1958 Constituency Assembly compelled Ezboni to join politics to realize his dream for the independence of South Sudan.. Thereafter his life and career, was determined by the political developments in the Sudan and Southern Sudan, starting with the first phase of forming a political party; successfully winning the elections on the party ticket; incarceration (jail) on trumped up charges; taking up a cabinet ministerial position in the transitional government of PM Sir El Khatim El Khalifa in 1964; and relief from that post following his lone action to save Southern Sudanese lives in Khartoum.

The second phase of Ezboni's eventful life was that began and which included; joining the Anyanya and making desperate efforts to reform the local Anyanya; assuming the vantage position as the Secretary of Defense of the Azania Liberation Front (ALF), under President Joseph Oduho; trekking the country to drum up support for the resistance movement, a feat which no other leaders of the movement undertook; commencing the unification of the Anyanya nationally and restructuring of the country administratively; facing a conspiracy and coup which ultimately killed his dream of building the movement; and finally escaping to exile in Uganda, after being sidelined and incarcerated by his very colleagues.

The third phase of Ezboni's struggle began when he was recalled by Joseph Lagu then President of the Movement, to head the Southern Sudan Liberation Movement (SSLM) delegation to the Addis Ababa peace talks which led to the establishment of the Southern Sudan Regional Government (SSRG). Here began a new life for Ezboni that included: as cabinet minister in the Southern Regional Government; through the rough and tumble of the intra-Southern Sudanese politics; and taking an uncompromising position against *kokora* and campaigning widely to stem it to save the Addis Ababa Agreement as well as the unity of the Southern Sudanese. The book shows that after *kokora*, Ezboni sat out of politics altogether because of his divergent views with the post-*kokora* divided Southern Sudan and also with the subsequent regime with National Islamic Front (NIF) led by Omar El Bashir. The book ends with an epitaph and demise and evaluation of the man who was Ezboni in which I had the privilege to contribute.

In going through the various episodes of his life as narrated above, one can clearly see the selfless devotion, Southern nationalism, determination, sacrifice to ultimately free his people, even when as it happened, he was rejected and humiliated by his people as well as sidelined by his very colleagues as it happened in the Angudri National Convention. Written chronologically, the book offers a great deal of knowledge about the overall vicissitudes and progress of the Southern Sudanese politics, and particularly a periscopic insight into the Southern Resistance Movement outside and of the Anyanya insurgents. Furthermore, the book adds substantially to many other books which have been written about that critical period of the history of South Sudan, especially, those written by his contemporaries like Abel Alier, Hilary Logali, Severino Fuli, Bona Malwal, Joseph Lagu and others. I highly recommend it to all South Sudanese, but especially to scholars who are interested to study more closely, that period of our history

At this point, I highly recommend this book to the South Sudanese public, and especially the scholars, and the keen watchers of South Sudan affairs, who wish to know something about Southern Sudan in that critical period 1954-1985 in the life of South Sudan; and finally, I would like to thank Professor

Peter Tingwa for giving me the opportunity to read and write the Foreword to this informative book.

- Dr. David S. Bassiouni
New York August 2023

Map 1: Provinces of the Anglo-Egyptian Sudan

Map 2: Amadi (Mundri) District (Today Greater Mundri and Counties)

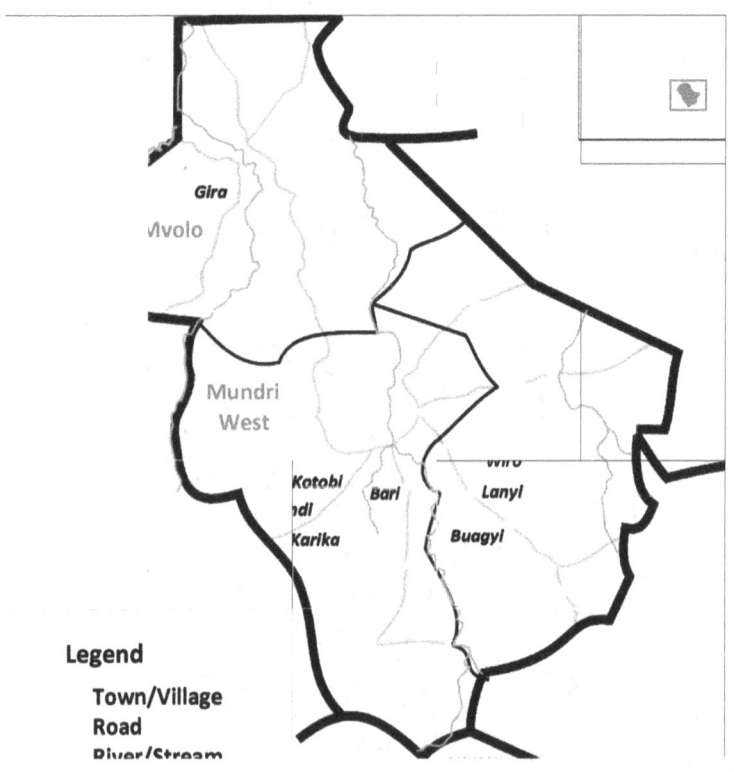

CHAPTER 1: INTRODUCTORY BACKGROUND

The Sudan, Historical and Contextual Perspective
Introduction

As a background to understanding as to how and why the South Sudanese and for that matter Ezboni Mondiri had to struggle to free themselves from domination by the Northern Sudanese, a brief history of how the entities of Sudan and Southern Sudan came into being is necessary, especially as to how Southern Sudan came to find itself at a disadvantage in that construct called the Sudan.

Generally it can be said that Southern Sudan has a history of double foreign rule by foreign rulers and by their compatriots in the north. Southern Sudan began when the Turco-Egyptian government invaded the Sudan from 1821 and created three provinces of Fashoda (Upper Nile), Equatoria and Bahr el Ghazal in the southern part of the country. However, they subjected the people to exploitation and slavery. In 1885, the Northern Sudanese under Mohamed Ahmed El Mahdi (Mahdists) overthrew the Turco-Egyptian government and established some rule over Southern Sudan as well. Their rule however did not differ much from that of the Turco-Egyptians before them; and so exploitation and slavery went on unabated. In fact, both the Egyptians and the Northern Sudanese regarded the Southern Sudanese as primitive people and infidels, only fit to be enslaved and sold; and for that reason, they had no qualms about taking them into slavery. As a consequence, that treatment engendered the enduring dislike and distrust of the Southern Sudanese towards the Egyptians and the Northern Sudanese.

Creating the Southern Sudan Entity and Differences

In 1898, the British using Egypt as a cover, defeated the Mahdists and in 1899, together with the Egyptians, established a joint (condominium) rule over the Sudan. The new country, the Anglo-Egyptian Sudan (Map 1) was however dominated by the British partner in the condominium arrangement. The country was divided into provinces, nearly following the set up under the Turco-Egyptian administration and, after several adjustments of the internal boundaries, the country eventually was divided into nine provinces: six in the northern part of the country and three in the southern part of the country.

But thereafter, while the six provinces in the north were immediately placed on a developmental trajectory after the signing the condominium agreement, the same was not done to the three provinces in the south. As no tangible reason could be found, that differential treatment could probably be due to the fact that many of the peoples of Southern provinces were resisting and continued to resist the condominium administration for a much longer time. Secondly, on noticing that the three Southern provinces differed markedly from the six Northern provinces, in terms of history, ethnicity, religion, culture, as well as ecologically, the condominium rulers decided to administer them differently from the six provinces in the north. That took a number of steps which were as follows: in 1917, they established the Equatoria Corps, constituted only of Southerners, ostensibly as a bulwark against a repeat of Islamism in the Sudanese army, which happened as happened during the Turco-Egyptian era[1]. In 1918, the rest day in Southern provinces was changed to Sunday; and in the same year, English was adopted to be the official language in the Southern provinces. In 1922, the Closed District Ordinance was promulgated, which restricted foreigners and Northern Sudanese to access the Southern provinces, and it also restricted the Southern Sudanese from going to the North.

Thirdly, in 1930, they enacted a policy, Southern Policy, encapsulating and reinforcing the Closed District Ordnance, ostensibly to prevent the spread of Islam and Arabism among the people of the south. Fourthly, as regards development of the south, they prescribed a policy and program of 'care and maintenance' only. That is, maintenance of law and order but no developmental activities.

In view of the above, and although the Anglo-Egyptian administration brought tranquility and stability in the South, the

---

1   During the Turco-Egyptian rule, the Sudanese soldiers in the Turco-Egyptian army joined Mahdism en messe, that eventually led to the fall of that regime.

cumulative effect of those policies and actions were that, while the Northerners became more enlightened, more politically conscious and more economically prosperous, the Southerners remained stagnant and undeveloped. That disparity in development and enlightenment further deepened the already existing differences and inequality between the North and the South. Hence, because they were already enlightened, the Northerners were able to catch on the wave and spirit of independence that was sweeping the Third World countries after the Second World War. As a consequence, they began to request the Condominium Government to grant independence to the Sudan. In their request for independence, they were supported by the Egyptians, the junior partners in the Condominium rule. In the end, the British (Condominium Government) relented to their demand of independence for the Sudan and, consequently, in 1946 it abandoned the Southern Policy through which Southern Sudan had been administered separately from Northern Sudan.

As the preparations for independence were growing in the North, the Southerners were not only totally unaware of those developments but were also ill-prepared for them politically. But when the information that the British (Condominium Government) would imminently depart began to filter among the Southerners, they became alarmed. They feared that, with the departure of the British, slavery and other bad deeds which they had received during the Turco-Egyptian and Mahdist (Northern Sudanese) era would return. That unpreparedness and fear of the Southerners were clearly seen by the British administrators in the South but, unfortunately, the British, Egyptians, the Northern Sudanese and the Condominium Government did not heed their concerns and pressed full throttle with preparations for the Sudan to be independent as a unitary state. That decision was concretised in the Sudan Administrative Conference (SAC) of January 1947[2] and here was where the Southern Sudanese were betrayed.

That decision upset many of the British administrators in the South, notably Deputy Governor Owen in Wau and District Commissioner of Yambio Major Wyld. Both felt strongly that the Southerners had been let down by the British and were now being forced into a unitary system with sophisticated Northerners and with no guarantees against their domination. They therefore proposed that the best guarantee for the Southern people against future Northern designs was a federation as was then being mooted for Malawi, Southern Rhodesia and Northern Rhodesia.

In June 1947, a palliative conference was convened in Juba by the Civil Secretary Sir James Robertson, ostensibly to sound the views of the Southerners about their joining the unitary legislative body in Khartoum; but it really was more to assuage those critical British administrators in the South than getting the views of the Southerners as to whether they want to live with the Northerners. Because, the decision for Southern representatives to go to the legislative assembly in Khartoum had already been taken and sealed earlier in the Sudan Administrative Conference in January. So, that Conference neither decided on the unity of Sudan, as the Northerners would want to believe nor on the Southern demand for federation as many Southerners still say today.

As was agreed in SAC, representatives of the Southerners

---

2   In that year, Bahr El Ghazal and Mongalla Provinces had been amalgamated to form one large province called Equatoria with the Governor resident in Juba and the Deputy resident in Wau.

went to the Legislative Assembly in Khartoum in 1948. However, what they were hearing from their Northern colleagues did not inspire trust and condence. The Northerners were talking of Arabization and Islamization in post-independent Sudan. In that atmosphere, the views of the few enlightened Southerners ranged from either wanting the Condominium Government to stay longer to bring them to be at par with the Northern Sudanese; separating Southern Sudan from the North to be a separate country; or partitioning the country to be two federal states, the North and the South.

From this apprehension and the disillusionment with the imminent independence of the Sudan, coupled with the replacement of British administrators in the South by Northern Sudanese officers, Southerners began to plan to extricate themselves from that predicament. Thus, there was a collusion between some of the politicians in Juba and some elements of the Equatoria Corps in Torit to do something about it. That collusion culminated in the 18 August 1955 uprising, led by the soldiers and which was joined by the policemen and the civilians, especially in Equatoria. That uprising was crushed but it rekindled the old spirit of resistance to foreign domination, which had been suppressed and had fallen dormant during the condominium era. It also engendered a stronger political resistance to the Northern Sudanese domination and set the stage for subsequent civil wars (resistance) in the Sudan and which only ended in 2011.

Southern Resistance to Foreign Rule

This book is about resumed Southern resistance to foreign rule and the role of one of its sons, Ezboni Mondiri Gwonza, in that resistance. It is that having lived free in their own world for many millennia, all the peoples of Southern Sudan put up resistance to the presence of the successive foreigners, be they Turco-Egyptians, Mahdists, the British combined with the Egyptians or the latter-day Northerners in post- independent Sudan. The struggle could be seen to have occurred in two phases: the first phase was resistance to foreign domination with no political objective as waged by tribal leaders like Gbudwe, Kon Anok, Dio Alam, Ariendit *et cetera*; and the second phase was the resistance to domination by the Northern Sudanese with a political objective of freedom and independence as waged by latter-day national leaders, beginning with leaders like Buth Diu, Paul Logali, Stanislaus Paysama, Benjamin Lwoki Eliya Kuze, Abdel Rahman Sule, and many others to the generation of Ezboni Mondiri, Joseph Oduho, Clement Mboro, William Deng, Hilary Logali, Fr. Saturnino, Gordon Mourtat. Joseph Lagu, Luigi Adwok and many more others. A few of those in the new leadership are shown in Plates III (a) to (l).

Ezboni Mondiri, through his contributions and sacrifices, certainly stands to be counted among those national leaders. Unfortunately, this fact has however been lost to many historians and writers on the Southern Sudanese political struggle for freedom. Often Ezboni's name is missing in the citations and listing of the leaders. This book is therefore aimed at bringing forth who the person Ezboni was, the roles he played and the challenges he faced in pursuing that struggle, as will be narrated in the subsequent chapters. Hopefully at the end, many South Sudanese will have been exposed to the life of a man who rightfully ranks amongst the founding fathers of the struggle for a free South Sudan, together with his contemporaries mentioned in this book. Now read on.

CHAPTER II:
THE FORMATIVE YEARS

Ezboni Mondiri Gwonza Seyi
Family Line, the Kari'ba Clan

The Moru tribe like any other is divided into clans or family clans. Usually those family clans, wherever they are found, have the same totems (*karo*) and custom (*la'bi*). The Kari'ba Clan into which Ezboni was born is one of the many family clans of the Moru tribe. Postulations are that, very long time ago, they lived in the general area of Diko, area of Chief Ngere, where some of them are still living today. But due either to intra-clan or family disharmony, coupled with pressure inside the Congo valley as a result of European incursion, some of them migrated northwards. In their northward movement, some settled in the area of Medeu; others settled in the area of Lozo and across River Mosa in Piri area; others went and settled in the Singo area; while more others proceeded, further north eastwards and settled in the Kädiro area. As of today, those who remained in the Diko area are recognized and consider themselves as Moru Ändri because they speak the Ändri dialect of the Moru language. Those who migrated and settled in Medeu, Lozo, Mosa, Piri and Singo areas are recognized and consider themselves as Moru Miza, because they speak the Miza dialect. While those who went furthest and settled in the Kädiro area (*Muku ya*) are recognized and consider themselves as Kädiro, because they speak the Kädiro dialect of the Moru language.

Ezboni's Family

Ezboni Mondiri's father Gwonza Seyi belonged to the Kari'ba Clan, the section that live in the area Piri Dri (literally meaning "On the White Wash", because of the presence of white and pink aluminum silicate deposits found there). As a young man, he joined the police force at Amadi, then a district of Mongalla Province. He took part in quelling the Aliab rebellion, under Chief Kon Anok, when in 1914 they killed the Governor of Mongalla Province, Major Chauncy Stigand. While at Amadi, he got married to Moroŋwa of the Kenyi Clan of Sub-Chief Ogyiŋwa. By then, Moroŋwa had two boys from a previous marriage, Bäni and Käyizele whom Gwonza adopted as his sons. In the new marriage, however, they bore three sons, respectively: Jose Seyi, Ezboni Mondiri and Maranyi. The exact year and date of Ezboni's birth are not known, but it could approximately be in the mid-1920s.

Sometimes later, Gwonza married a second wife, Naomi Nagyi from Mide Clan of the 'Bäṛi'ba Section of the Moru tribe and they had five children, respectively, Awa, Charles Jato,

Plate I: Ezboni Mondiri Gwonza

Elizara Gyima, Christopher Lemeri and Charity Lorna. Thus, in addition to his two sibling brothers, Ezboni had two sets of half-brothers and sisters one from his mother and the other set from his step mother.

As for his own family, after graduation in 1954, Ezboni got married to Nurse Elizabeth Tombiŋwa Abarayama from Lakama'di and they had four children: three girls and one boy, Florence May, Sara June, Kyila and Lenin Tataŋwa. In 1973, Ezboni got married to a second wife Eva Elisa from Ma'di Clan, near 'Buägyi. They bore seven children and they were Malish, Maranyi, Jami, Kenyi, Thomas, Nyango and Emmanuel.

Plate II: Ezboni's Wife Elizabeth Tombiŋwa Abarayama

Education

Elementary Schooling

When Gwonza retired from police service, he came back home and built a home about three kilometers west of Lanyi, the chief's village. From there, Ezboni entered school in what then was called Bush or Out School at Lanyi. In 1940, he completed Classes 1 and 2 at Lanyi and like 150 other bush school finalists, he had to sit an entrance examination in order to be admitted to the 30-space Class 3 of the Lui Elementary Vernacular School. He passed those examinations and was among the few who were selected to join Class 3 of the Lui Elementary Vernacular School.

During those two years, his colleagues say, he began to develop a lot of the traits that later would characterize his personality in adult life, that is, forth- rightness and independence.

At the end of 1942, he completed Class 4 and took the entrance examination for admission to intermediate level education at the Nugent School at Loka. It was the primiere Church Missionary Society (CMS) School in Southern Sudan. Loka was thus the mecca and goal of every pupil in all the CMS elementary schools. So, in order to get admitted to the only 30 places in Loka, one had to pass a stringent examination and compete with all Class 4 finalists in all the CMS elementary schools in Southern Sudan. Ezboni passed those examinations very well and was among the few pupils who were selected to enter the school in 1942.

At Nugent (Intermediate) School, Loka

Loka was a great place for learning, knowing people from the other tribes and making friends. At Loka, Ezboni's academic performance continued to be very good. He was always among the top students in his class in the four years he was in that school. At the same time, his leadership qualities, independent-mindedness and ability for making quick decisions were becoming increasingly evident and well defined. Furthermore, he would not suffer fools. For that reason, according to Elinana Were and Yezenaya Jaraba, his school mates, he was fondly and sometimes grudgingly nicknamed 'Mäfä' by his school mates. In the final year, he obtained very good grades, sufficient for admission to secondary level education. But in those years, there were no secondary schools in Southern Sudan because the

Government did not open any. Furthermore, it also prevented the missionary societies from opening any for the Southern Sudanese. So, intermediate school level of learning was the highest the Southerners could get in those years.

However, the Government did allow the missionaries to send the best students from the intermediate schools of Loka, Okaru and Bussere to go for secondary education to Uganda. In that respect, the Catholic schools of Bussere and Okaru sent their best students to Nyapea Secondary School. Some of the students they sent were Louis Buok, Roman Hassan, Caesar Loleya and others. On the other hand, the Anglican (CMS) sent their best students from Loka to either Makerere Secondary School in Kampala or Nabumali High School in Mbale. Those who were sent to Uganda before Ezboni included individuals like Michael Dafalla, Michael Wata, Eliaba Ginaba Toto, Aggrey Jaden, John Garang, Bullen Alier and others.

In Nabumali High School in Uganda

In 1947, Ezboni was accepted to Nabumali High School, together with contemporaries like Zakaria Wani Yugusuk, Elia Lupe and Frederick Magot Daŋgoro. In that school, the students from Southern Sudan (Loka) not only proved to be very good academically but they also excelled in sport, athletics and football For example, while students like Eliaba Toto and Zakaria Wani excelled in football and short distance running, Ezboni, excelled in middle distance running. In that way, they made Nabumali High to be one of the topmost schools in sport in Uganda.

But, while he was in the school in Uganda, Ezboni noticed

two striking things, which were different from what he was used to in Southern Sudan. He noticed that in Uganda, the European (British) teachers and others associated and socialized freely with the Ugandans; that is, they could visit the Ugandans in their homes, share conversations with them and even eat the Ugandan foods. They also could invite the Ugandans to their homes for the same. That was in sharp contrast to the situation in Southern Sudan, where the Europeans, missionaries or government officials alike, rarely socialized with the South Sudanese or ate their foods; even if the food was hygienically prepared and clean. Another striking thing he saw was that the Ugandans, who were just like the South Sudanese, were occupying fairly senior administrative positions in their government, whereas in the Sudan, the Southern Sudanese were only occupying junior posts, such as clerks, bookkeepers and so on. Those observations were later to shape his thinking about the British and the low regard they had for the South Sudanese in the Sudan. In fact, those observations made him to be an ardent critic of the British rule in Southern Sudan. At the end of his schooling at Nabumali in 1950, Ezboni took the Cambridge Ordinary Level Examinations and obtained a very good grade, enough to admit him to a university.

In the Gordon Memorial University College of Khartoum

Thus in 1951, like Aggrey Jaden, John Garang and Louis Buok before him, was accepted to the Faculty of Arts in the Gordon Memorial University College of Khartoum, which then was affiliated to the University of London. He thus became the fourth South Sudanese ever to access university level education.

It was in the University that Ezboni's political views were shaped by what he experienced in the institution as well as by the political developments that were then going on around him in the Sudan at the time.

Waking up Politically

In the University, apart from the academic and intellectual learning, Ezboni's political views conviction and stand began to take shape from his interaction with fellow students as well as from the politics going on in Khartoum. For the first time, he was exposed to the Northern people, their mentality, culture, political views and commitments. Coming as he did from secluded Southern Sudan and Uganda, most of their views were in sharp contrast to what he was used to. Outside the University, political agitation for independence was very high and the debate as to whether the Sudan should unite with Egypt after independence (Ashigga Party) or be an independent country (Umma Party) was also high. As those debates went on, Ezboni saw that the people of the South had been taken for granted. Their interests, aspirations and indeed their presence in the country did not even cross the minds of the debaters.

In the University, the student politics was also similarly divided. There were the conservative traditionalists, who paid allegiance to the religious sects of the Ansar (Umma) and the Khatmiya (Peoples Democratic Party); and there were the liberals who comprised of the independents, socialists and communists. Given those political divisions in the student body, the handful of Southern students in the University allied themselves to the liberals/socialists/communists, rather than to the sectarian traditionalists. But they were not members of any of the components of the group. This alliance however was misunderstood by the missionaries, who thought that the Southern students in the University had all become communists![3] This allegation, as we shall see much later, was used in the plot against Ezboni in the Azania Liberation Front (ALF) that he was a communist. As the case was, that alliance of the Southern students with the liberals and socialists in the University continued until the late 1950s, when after their numbers had increased in the University, they formed their own student party, the Students Welfare Front (SWF). The SWF was strongly southern oriented in its political outlook.

According to Ezboni, while he was still in the University, two issues had indelible effect on him and that those issues shaped his political views and convictions. Firstly, coming as he did from Uganda, where he was seen and taken for what he was, and also of the fact that in Uganda, where the black Africans were doing things for themselves, Ezboni was shocked to note that in the Sudan, both the British and the Northerners had very low esteem for the Southern Sudanese and spoke condescendingly to and about them. He encountered this view and mentality several times in his interactions with fellow Northern Sudanese students and he detested it. This was in marked contrast to the way he was regarded and treated in Uganda, a supposedly foreign country.

Secondly, in the politics going on in and out of the University, the viewpoint of the South Sudanese did not even cross the minds of the discussants of the independence of the Sudan. It was such that the British, the Egyptians and the Northern Sudanese had

---

3	Hilary Logali in his book 'In the Struggle' also mentions the same.

connived and had railroaded the Southerners, *fait accompli,* into a united Sudan. In this, Ezboni's disappointment and anger was directed more at the British for under-developing the Southern Sudanese and also for treating them as inferior second-class citizens (lower pay for same work). He also detested the callous way by which they were handing over the South Sudanese willy-nilly to the Northern Sudanese.

Both of these combined to shape Ezboni's political convictions and made him the Southern nationalist he was. Ezboni thus became a vocal defender of Southern interests and also of their freedom from the North. His vocal, open and strong view was that Southern Sudan should out rightly be separated from Northern Sudan by the British and his Northern colleagues were fully aware of his views. They therefore considered him as an extremist and a separatist, which they felt were inimical to the independence and future of the Sudan. This Northern view of Ezboni persisted and, as it will be seen later, affected his later political life.

Embracing Federation

Ezboni's stand for outright independence for Southern Sudan came to be modified, when Mr. Faustino Roro, an official of the Equatoria Province Board (EPB) in Nzara and who had been sensitized by Major Wyld of Yambio about federation, visited them, the Southern Students, in the University of Khartoum. Roro apprised them of the idea of federation as a solution for protecting the Southerners from Northern Sudanese domination. So from that day, rather than outright separation, which was already difficult to attain at that time, he embraced federation but as a stepping step to gaining full separation.

Compelling Reasons for Joining Politics

By now 1953, federation had become a demand for the Southern politicians. Having embraced it as a political objective, Ezboni's problem was now about how to effect it. From the close quarters in the University of Khartoum he knew that, as novices in politics, Southern nominated members in 1948-1953 Legislative Assembly were unable to articulate it. He similarly was dissatisfied with the performance of the subsequent elected members of the 1953 Parliament (the Liberal Party), led by Chairman Benjamin Lwoki. He came to realize that, though the Party had adopted federation as their prime demand, they too were not articulating the demand very well. That view dawned on him when he volunteered as a personal assistant to Chairman Benjamin Lwoki and had the chance to see the inner workings of the Liberal Party at close quarters. Ezboni was also disappointed with the Party because they were unable to express other Southern grievances and aspirations, such as due consideration for Southerners in the Sudanization program that was then going on. Furthermore, Ezboni was disappointed with the way in which some of them were handling themselves in the Assembly, like being bought right and left by the Northern political parties. What hurt him most was to see some of them preferring to join the Northern political parties, rather than stand with their brothers in the demand for federation

It was from those reasons, and while still in the University, that Ezboni decided to be a politician in order to effect federation and speak and stand for Southern Sudan and its people. To him, the South Sudanese people had been betrayed by the British and so, without any safeguards, were about to be handed over to be devoured by the Northern Sudanese. He therefore was determined to fight to prevent it. So, in the student circles, his stand for federalism for future Sudan were open and very much known to his Northern colleagues and which they considered inimical to the impending independence of the Sudan. As a consequence, they took Ezboni to be a very dangerous person to the future of the country. For that reason, many of them have held this view of him from those student days, right through his political career in later life.

Working Life After Graduation

In 1954, Ezboni graduated from the University. But rather than join the abundant senior government posts that were being vacated by the departing British civil servants under the Sudanization Program, Eiboni chose employment with the Shell Oil Company. His employment in Shell Company enabled him to travel to many parts of the country. Sometime later, Ezboni was made the Regional Director of the Shell Company operations in Southern Sudan. In that capacity, he immediately embarked on expanding and modernizing Shell Company operations in Southern Sudan. Consequently, Shell Company began constructing fuel pumps along the major roads and in towns like Torit, Juba, Yei, Mundri, Maridi, Yambio, Wau, and Rumbek. A pump station was to have been constructed at Lainya but that did not come into being because Ezboni left the Company to join politics

In Shell Company, he was to find another Southerner, Mr. Darius Beshir, a Fertit and a graduate of Khartoum Technical Institute who also did not bother to join government employment.

The two were to found a political association in which Darius became Ezboni's right hand man. Ezboni's assignment required him to travel all over the Sudan. In one of those travels in the country, he traveled to Port Sudan, where he met Morris Ägyili Kayanga, who was working as a clerk in the Sudan Railways. The two also hit off immediately, especially in respect to their political views. Morris, as will be seen later, became Ezboni's confidant, special assistant, chief campaign manager and shared many of Ezboni's political vicissitudes and life. It is thus appropriate at this stage to review the political situation in Southern Sudan into which Ezboni was soon to plunge.

The Then Prevailing Political Situation in Southern Sudan
Southern Political Awakening and the First Resistance

The political situation in Southern Sudan, just before Ezboni plunged into politics, was as follows. The Parliament that was elected in 1953 was extant and Ismail El Azhari of the National Unionist Party was the Prime Minister (PM) of the Self Government. The British Governor General was still the head of the state. Sudanization of political and administrative posts was underway but many British administrators were still holding their posts, especially in Southern Sudan, However, by this time, Southerners had become more politically aware and restive than before. There, however, was a general apprehension about life after independence, that is, after the British had left. Hence, the idea of federation for the Sudan, earlier floated by Major Wyld and colleagues, had caught on among educated Southerners as a panacea or bulwark against future Northern designs.

In October 1954, in a meeting in Juba the Liberal Party had adopted federation for Southern Sudan as its prime objective. In June 1955, the Liberal Party called a conference of Southerners to which the Southern NUP members were invited. The then Self- Government of PM Ismail El Azhari and the Northerners in general were alarmed when they came to learn that the Southern NUP members were going to attend it. They also became aware of the growing discontent among the Southerners against the impending independence as well as of the Southerners' wish for the British to stay longer. Furthermore, they had the suspicion that there was a collusion between the Southern officials, the Liberal Party, remnants of the British officers in the South and the Equatoria Corps in Torit to jeopardize the impending independence of the country. Therefore, PM Ismail El Azhari's Government took a mission to Southern Sudan to shore up the image of the government and also rally support for unity and independence of the country. He however was badly received in both Malakal and Juba. In Juba, Daniel Jumi walked out of the meeting and was followed by the rest of the attendants and for this, he was marked as an agitator. PM Azhari therefore took actions to thwart those developments. Those actions included: the mass transfer of Southern officials to the North; the arrest of the so-called agitators, Daniel Jumi, Frazer Ako and Marko Rume in Juba; the arrest and sentencing of MP Eliya Kuze and consequent riot and killing of civilians in Yambio and Nzara; the arrest of 2nd Lt Taffeng Lodongi; and finally, the attempt to disarm the No. 2 Company in Torit on 18 August 1955.

The 18 August Uprising

Unfortunately, those actions only served to exacerbate the situation. Consequently, on 18 August 1955, they led to a full-scale uprising against the Government in Equatoria, led by the members of the Equatoria Corps. The uprising covered the whole Province and many people, especially Northerners, were killed. In fact, the rebellion was such that for more than two weeks, the Government in Khartoum and Juba lost control of the whole of Equatoria Province, except for the town of Juba. But although Southern Sudan was now virtually under their control, unfortunately, the Equatoria Corps Torit soldiers failed to use that opportunity politically and militarily. They failed to keep their command structure as well as to consolidate their gains. Furthermore, they failed to voice as well as articulate their political demands.

In response, PM Ismail El Azhari successfully used the newly arrived British Governor General, Sir Alexander Knox Helm, to persuade the rebels to surrender and they did so without a *quid pro quo*. They naively trusted the Governor General because he was British. In the meantime, the Government, using British Royal Air Force aircraft sent Northern troops to replace the Equatoria Corps which later was disbanded.

Repercussions of the Uprising

After the surrender of the soldiers, the reprisals by Government of Ismail El Azhari were very brutal. It was undertaken in the name of restoring law and order. Many people were arrested and tortured and the Equatoria Corp was disbanded. Several kangaroo courts were established, which summarily tried and condemned the soldiers, policemen and many ordinary people to either death or long-term prison sentences. Non-Commissioned Officer (NCO) Renaldo Loleya, who led the Torit soldiers, himself was shot and Second Liutenant Taffeng was jailed, while NCO Ali Gbatala and others escaped to the forest. In the trials, several civilians like Samuel Kajivora, Bullen Ngangi, Michael Wata and many others were also executed. Other civilians like Joseph Oduho, Lewis Gore, among many others were jailed.

As should be expected, the over-reaction by El Azhari's Government in suppressing the uprising further embittered the Southern Sudanese against the Government as well as against Northerners in general. Consequently, many of the ex-soldiers like Lotada Hilir in Imatong Mountains; Ali Gbatala in the forests of Maridi; Tadayo Lasuba near Yei; Philip near Kapoeta; and others fled to the forests to continue the fight. After his release from jail in 1961, Second Lt. Taffeng Lodongi also took to the Imatong Mountains to continue the fight.

Those repercussions worked to convince the Southerners of their misgivings and fears of living in harmony with Northerners in an independent Sudan. In hindsight, if the British and the Northerners had seriously taken that uprising as a warning sign of things to come; and had done something to genuinely address the grievances, perhaps Southern discontent would not have eventually led to the break-up of Sudan. Instead, the British washed their hands off the Sudan and left; and the Northerners took to political suppression, Islamization and Arabization.

On the other hand, in assessing the success/failure of this uprising/rebellion the following can be said: i) had the soldiers in Torit not disintegrated as a result of poor leadership; ii) had they acted in unison with their colleagues in Wau, Malakal and other towns; and iii) if they had some good political leadership, they could have consolidated their control over the South and bargained for a better status/relationship with the North, even when matters regarding the status of the Sudan had already been sealed. As McCall says in his book, the uprising/rebellion *"suffered from crippling lack of leadership"*, adding that *"In fact, all the problems of Southern liberation movement from 1955 to this day has been the lack of leadership"*

Sudan Becomes Independent

Another eventful occurrence before Ezboni's joining of politics was the independence of the Sudan on 01 January 1956. As per the Cairo Agreement in 1953, independence was to have been voted for in a plebiscite. However, PM Azhari and the Northern political parties changed tack for independence to be voted for by the Legislative Assembly in December 1955. They were well aware that, if the Southern Liberal Party demand for federation had not been addressed, the Southern members might not vote for independence. So they deceived the Southern members, saying that the issue of federation would be given full consideration after independence. The Southern members naively believed them and so on 19 December 1955 they voted together with the Northerners for the Sudan to be independent on 01 January 1956. That was too soon for many Southerners.

On that material day, there was much joy and celebrations about it in the North but in the South, there was no joy, especially in Equatoria, since it coincided with the time, when many of those who were suspected to have committed atrocities during the uprising were being tried. Thus, many Southerners opted not to celebrate the day. In Khartoum, Ezboni did not go out celebrating it; and Assistant District Commissioner, Aggrey Jaden, also did not go to witness the raising of the flag of the independent Sudan, and for that reason, he was promptly dismissed from service.

CHAPTER III:
TAKING THE PLUNGE
INTO POLITICS

Decision and Gearing up for Politics

As those events were happening in Southern Sudan, Ezboni was in Khartoum and he watched them with a heavy heart. Like his other colleagues of the better educated and newer generation of Southern elites, the 1955 Uprising and the ensuing repercussion reinforced his decision and commitment to join politics in order to fight for Southern freedom. Some of those colleagues, who will be mentioned in the subsequent paragraphs, are shown below in Plates III (a) to III (l).

Thus, having taken the decision, Ezboni began to work on the formation of a political party, solely devoted to the winning of federation and ultimately separation for Southern Sudan.

Plate III (a) to (l): Contemporaries of Ezboni in the Struggle

Plate III (a): Ezboni Mondiri Gwonza   *Plate III (b): Aggrey Jaden Lado*   *Plate III (C): Fr. Saturnino Ohure*

Politics of the Permanent Constitution for the Sudan

In 1957, the life of the 1953 Legislative Assembly came to an end and new elections were scheduled to take place in early 1958 for the Constituent Assembly. As the case was, that Assembly was going to be a very critical one for the country, since it was expected to write the permanent constitution. Thus, the stakes were very high. For the Northerners, the Islamic sectarian parties, Umma and DUP, it was important because they wanted the permanent constitution which would reflect the Islamic nature of the country. On the other hand, for the Southerners it was the opportunity to incorporate federation into the permanent constitution and for it to be a secular one. But this wish for federal status for the Sudan was very much rejected by

Plate III (d):
William Deng Nhial

Plate III (e):
Joseph Oduho Haworu

Plate III (f):
Clement Mboro

Plate III (g):
Gordon Mourtat

Plate III (h):
Joseph Lagu Yanga

Plate III (i): Abel Alier Kwai

Plate III (j):
Hilary Paul Logali

Plate III (k):
Gismalla Abdalla Rassas

Plate III (l): Joseph James Tambura

all Northerners. Deep down, Ezboni like many other educated Southerners at the time, believed in the separation of the South from the North. However, given what had already transpired many had come to the conclusion that, federation was the only option, if only temporarily.

Ezboni Forms the Federal Party

Ezboni saw that this was the right time for him to join politics if at all his dream to have federation for Southern Sudan was to be included in the permanent constitution. Ezboni could have joined the Liberal Party which also was advocating for federation. He however conceived the formation of a party that could better articulate the Southern demand for federation. He came upon this conviction from his observation of the Liberal Party, when as a student in the university, he worked with the Liberal Party Chairman, Benjamin Lwoki. He thus came to doubt the capacity of the Liberal Party to achieve federation for the South. Ezboni therefore decided to form the Federal Party[4] which, like the Liberal Party, also advocated for a federal status for Southern Sudan in one Sudan. He was assisted in this by Darius Beshir and also by then Captain Zakaria Wani Yugusuk, another graduate of the Khartoum Technical Institute who was in the army. They began to canvas for his party and the party came to be supported by many younger and better educated Southerners as well as Southern workers in Khartoum such as Musa Bily, Hassan Beshir and others.

---

4   Several writings say that Ezboni formed the Federal Party together with Fr Saturnino. That is not correct. He formed it with his colleagues in Khartoum.

Plate IV: Morris Ägyili Kayanga

By 1957, Ezboni's house in the Deims was a hive of activities. As the number of supporters grew, a cipher was invented for keeping the minutes of the meetings of the group. It was at this time that Mr. Morris Ägyili, whom he had earlier met in Port Sudan left his government employment and came to Khartoum to work with him.

Ezboni and group then prepared a charter of a federal system of governance for the Sudan. In the charter, he spelt out how the two federal states of the North and of the South, would be governed politically and economically. That was in marked contrast to the Liberal Party that lacked the capacity to spell out the details of the federation they were calling for. Unfortunately, a copy of the charter or manifesto was not available to the writer but a paraphrasing of it by Dr. John Gai Nyout Yoh can be found in Appendix I to give an idea of what it was.

After completing the Party's constitution, he sent copies for information to the three Southern Provinces: to Marko Rume in Juba, Dominic Muorwel in Wau and a Mr. Louis in Malakal. Many Southern federalists, including those in the Liberal Party, like Fr. Saturnino Ohure accepted the constitution and in fact treated it as if it were for their Party. This is in such contrast today, where Southern political parties, even when their objectives are the same, would fight bitterly against one another. For example, even when the objective of SPLM-IO and NAS are the same, that is to remove Salva and institute reforms, they have been fighting bitterly among themselves. In this, it would appear that the politicians of that generation were more nationalistic and had a higher moral stature than of the current generation.

In 1957, Ezboni registered the Party, with himself as the President and Darius Beshir as the Secretary General. Soon the new party caught interest and support of the many Southern officials in Khartoum. It also won the support of the Southern students in the University of Khartoum as well as of those in the secondary schools of Rumbek and Juba Commercial; both of which were then functioning in Khartoum at that time. Members began to make donations to the Party and an office was opened. Soon, interest in the new party spread to Southern officials in Wad Medani, where a branch was formed with Mr. Constantine Libra as the President, Mr. Severino Fuli as the Secretary General and Mr. Elisapa Ginaba as the Treasurer. As can be seen now, the party existed in the North only and its membership was largely composed of Southern intellectuals.

The 1958 General Elections for the Constituent Assembly
Preparing for the Elections

As the elections neared, Ezboni began to write the manifesto for the party. As Ezboni drafted the manifesto, Morris typed them. The original draft of the manifesto included a clause which never became part of the platform and which McCall describes as, quote: *"federation would be sought by legal means* (in the constituent assembly) *but should this fail, then other methods would be used. That is, a unilateral declaration of independence to be declared by the Southern members of the parliament, and if necessary, force would be used to defend it even if that would plunge the country into civil war"* As it will be seen later, that sentence in Ezboni's own hand writing was found by the security agents in his home and was used to convict him later. Unfortunately, no copies of Ezboni's papers are available today as they were all collected by the police at that time.

It is likely that it was during this period that Ezboni also engaged in some kind of psychological campaign to frighten the Northerners, especially the administrators in the South. Though he was not in contact with the hold-outs of the ex-Torit soldiers, he used to write some threatening letters to the Northern officials in Equatoria in the names of either Lotada, Taffeng, Ali Gbatala and/or others. Those papers were also found by the security in his home and they added to the evidences that convicted him, as we shall see later.

Strategizing for the Election

The elections were scheduled to take place at the end of 1957 to the beginning of 1958. In middle of 1957, Ezboni resigned his post in Shell Company to pursue his dream of a federal system for the Sudan. While living in the Deims suburb, south of Khartoum, he and his colleagues met every Friday to work out the party's manifesto and the campaign strategy. Ezboni's aim was to be elected on the Federal Party's ticket, through contesting the elections in his home base, that was, Constituency Number 4 (Amadi). Under Morris Ägyili, preparations of his campaign literature began in earnest, using his own money from his Shell Company gratuity. He travelled to Juba and explained his party's goals and avoided creating differences between his party and the Liberal Party establishment in Juba. Many people who met him or read his manifesto accepted his Federal Party program. While in Juba, he established a few agents such as, Eliaba Alau Rubä, Eliaba Ginaba Toto and a few others. He then proceeded home for the nominations.

All the while Ezboni knew he was going to go up against three other candidates: the incumbent representative, Chief Timon Biro Mbäriŋwa who was his own chief. Timon was a popular local chief and member of the Liberal Party and was a person of a clean record, both administratively and politically, and was much admired by his people. Ezboni did not have anything against the Chief, after all, the Liberal Party in which the Chief was standing was also calling for federation. However, as the time for nominations came, and seeing that Ezboni was a better person to address the then political situation, Chief Timon opted out of the election. The second candidate to the competition was Ezboni Jo'di. He stepped into the Liberal Party shoes when the Chief opted out. The third contestant was Zakaria Ligyigo Jambo, the son of Chief Jambo. He was standing for the National Unionist Party of Ismail El Azhari. Thus, there were three contestants for Constituency No. 4. They were: Ezboni Mondiri, Federal Party, with the symbol the axe; Ezboni Jo'di, Liberal Party, with the symbol of the head of sorghum (*dura*); and Zakaria Ligyigo, National Unionist Party, with the symbol of the hut. It is worth noting here that, all over Southern Sudan,

Ezboni was the only candidate who was contesting that election in his Federal Party.

Nomination and Campaign Message

After nominating himself, Ezboni came back to Khartoum to organize his campaign, together with Morris. Ezboni conducted a modern campaign, the like of which was not done by any previous politicians in the South. In Khartoum, with the assistance of Morris, he prepared slogans, flyers with his election symbol in both English and Moru language. The main message in the pamphlets was:

Mivo vodo koloŋwa ri ayani	Vote for the axe
Tana koloŋwa 'do si	Because, with the axe
Nya oye a'doni drìtayi ro	You will find freedom

He then requested the Moru officials and Moru students of Rumbek Secondary and Juba Commercial Secondary Schools, who at that time were in Khartoum, to supply the names of as many opinion-makers as possible from the localities from which they came in Moru land. Thereafter, each of those names were sent an envelope addressed to them and containing the campaign pamphlets. The letters and campaign materials were flown to Juba and sent to Moru land. The envelopes had a tremendous effect on the recipients, many of whom had never received letters in their lives from anywhere, least of all from Khartoum! Those recipients became instant campaign agents for Ezboni as they went around proudly displaying their letters which they had received all the way from Khartoum. His flyers and symbol were distributed very widely in Moru land and could be seen pasted on many prominent trees.

Campaigning on the Ground

On the ground, Morris was the main campaign manager. He stationed himself at Mundri. Morris was joined by Ismail Rajab, a tailor and very eloquent person who had lived in Khartoum and who knew the Arabic language and Northerners very well. His political views were the same as Ezboni's and Morris' views. Ezboni's style of campaign was to identify and use agents, not chiefs, as many other politicians were wont to do. Those agents were usually eloquent opinion- makers in their localities, who did most of the talking to the people. The thrust of Ezboni's campaign message was federation so that the Southerners could enjoy some degree of freedom from the domineering Northerners. He consistently preached to the people to be wary of Northern machinations and bribery, citing examples of how the earlier Southern politicians had succumbed to bribery at the expense of the interest and aspirations of the people of Southern Sudan. Ezboni told the people that he would not give money to anyone in order to get his or her vote, nor would he take bribes, especially from the Northerners. He told them that, if elected in the Parliament, he would present their wish for a greater freedom without fear. Furthermore, Ezboni and his agents made use of his symbol, the axe, for sending home his message.

Among the Moru people, the axe is considered to be one of the key tools of a man. It was such that, when a man was going out to the wilderness or the unknown; or things have come to a head and he longs for independence and freedom, as a courageous act, he usually would take a bow and arrows, a spear and an ax slung over his shoulder and venture into the unknown. So, Ezboni's campaigners were telling the people that, they should vote for the axe as a courageous act so as to venture into freedom and independence. As mentioned earlier, Ezboni's campaign was also enhanced by those who received the envelopes from Khartoum with the campaign literature. With a good level of literacy in the constituency, the message was read by a large section of the population. Moreover, in their excitement and show-off, those who received the envelopes distributed the campaign message very widely. All those created a whirl wind support in favor of Ezboni.

It is worth mentioning here that, during the campaign period, Ezboni campaigned across the Moru country and wherever he went, he took rest with relatives, friends or agents. At Lui, which served as one of his operational bases, he stayed and kept his campaign materials in his cousin, Obodaya Tingwa's house.

Other Competing Candidates

In the meantime, his rival candidates were also busy conducting their campaigns. The second candidate Ezboni Jo'di of the Liberal Party, whose symbol was the 'head of sorghum'(*dura*), was also campaigning for federation. He was telling the people to vote for the head of sorghum because it was food and that no one could live without food. The third candidate Zakaria Ligyigo Jambo of NUP had 'the hut' as his symbol and was campaigning for the unity of the Sudan. He was asking the people to vote for 'the hut' as it was the hut that gives shelter to the people in times of danger, rain or heat. He was also telling the people about the advantages of unity with the Northerners. However, Zakaria's candidacy and campaign faced two serious handicaps: Firstly, he was standing for a Northern political party, which the people did not like, especially with his message of unity with the Northerners. Secondly, as a son of Chief Jambo, who was a pro-Northerner and pro-Egyptian person, many people were just against him for that reason. Hence, the contest was really between the two Ezbonis, Mondiri and Jo'di. However, soon it became clear that Ezboni Mondiri's campaign was the most effective and that it was clear that he was going to win the election and therefore go to the Parliament.

Northern Connivance Against Ezboni

At his juncture, if there was anything the Northerners detested, it was to see Ezboni in the Parliament, since they knew his person as well as his political views from the student days, regarding federation and Southern Sudan. They therefore thought of doing anything possible that would prevent him from entering the Parliament. In fulfillment of that aim, the District Commissioner at Maridi, Abbas Fagiri, was probably instructed by his superiors in Juba and Khartoum to keep an eye on Ezboni, and possibly work out ways of how to prevent Ezboni from going to the Parliament. Fagiri therefore deployed informers and security officers to dog Ezboni's campaigns. It would appear that Ezboni had an inkling of the government's designs against him. Allegedly, one of the informers was a convert to Islam who was a junior clerk at Maridi. He was facilitated to travel to Khartoum and while there, he visited Ezboni's house in the

Deims which was then a beehive of activities of the Federal Party. As a familiar person, he interacted freely with the people in the office. McCall alleges that it probably was at this time that he caught a glimpse of Ezboni's drafts on Morris' table about using force in case federation was not going to be achieved peacefully through the Parliament. He also probably got a glimpse of Ezboni's drafts to Taffeng and Lotada. He returned to the South and gave his report to Abbas Fagiri and who requested him to continue to follow Ezboni's campaigns and report Ezboni's messages to the people to him. However by this time, DC Abbas Fagiri was now armed with information against Ezboni and was only waiting for a suitable time to strike.

Victory, Arrest, Escape and Re-Arrest
Arrest

When Omdurman Radio announced the results, Ezboni had won an overwhelming majority of the votes. He immediately wanted to go to Juba in order to travel to Khartoum with the other winners. But before he went to Lanyi to catch a vehicle to Juba, a police vehicle arrived from Amadi with several policemen on it. Ezboni's hunch that the Government would arrest him had come true. They arrested him and put him in the car, with the instruction to take him to the District Headquarters at Maridi. He was not handcuffed. And so as they passed Lanyi and Lui, many people saw Ezboni on the vehicle with the police. They wondered as to why. A few thought that because he was now the Parliamentarian-elect, he was being taken to the district headquarters for some honorary function. But many saw something more sinister, that is, Ezboni was being taken to Maridi as an accused person because the Government (Northerners) did not like what he was saying and what he stood for.

Escape

At early evening, around 4:00 pm, the police and Ezboni reached Mundri. They stopped in front of the shop of the Greek merchant, George. At that point, Ezboni asked the police to allow him to enter the shop to buy something. The police agreed. He alighted and went into the shop. While inside the shop, he asked Yanni, the Greek brother-in- law of George that he wanted to go to the toilet. Yanni opened the back door of the shop and showed him the toilet which was in the fence behind the shop. Once outside in the fence, Ezboni slipped out through the eastern gate of the fence and walked very briskly to the Government orange orchard along River Mori. He crossed Mori and then River Yei and walked through the forest towards Lui. Ezboni's aim was to go to Juba where he would be out of reach of Abbas Fagiri, because in Juba, the chances of him being lynched or otherwise would be less, given the international presence in Juba.

Back in the car and after waiting for a while, the police went inside the shop to request Ezboni so that they could proceed to Maridi. They were told that Ezboni was in the toilet behind the house. They went out into the fence behind the shop. But Ezboni was neither in the fence nor in the toilet. It immediately dawned on them that Ezboni had escaped. They searched the area around the orchard and the homesteads across River Mori, but could not find him. They then radioed Amadi and Maridi about this and the latter ordered a full search for Ezboni. As it was already dark, they decided to continue the search the next day, focusing on four spots: his cousin Obodaya's house at Lunjini, his sister-in-law Damari's house also at Lunjini, his home at Piri Dri and his father-in- law Abarayama Gyikaa's home at Lakama'di.

In the meantime, Ezboni arrived Obodaya's house at Lunjini at around 8:00 pm when it was already dark so none of the neighbors saw him. He told Obodaya's family about what had happened and instructed them to right away destroy all documents, campaign materials, including his personal letters because, he warned, the police would be coming searching for such documents. He also told them to deny ever seeing him that night. He was given food and requested to be given a bed in the open verandah of the house. While Ezboni rested, Obodaya and family began to destroy all documents relating to him. After resting and at around 4:00 am, Ezboni left and went to his home using the bush path behind the hills (Iro). He arrived home by 6.00 am; and same as he had done at Obodaya's house, he asked his brothers and sisters to destroy all documents and letters relating to him and deny ever seeing him after his arrest. Ezboni then went and hid under the thick mango trees on the western side of the homestead. Unfortunately, his brothers did not open some of Ezboni's big boxes.

The Search

As expected, at around 8:30 am, the police arrived at Obodaya's house, led by the General Service Officer (Mamur), Komoyangi Äbäbä. (NB: Note that at that time, the district headquarters had been transferred to Maridi, and the Moru area was thus under a General Service Officer at Amadi. Later, that office was transferred to Mundri). They asked if Obodaya's family had seen Ezboni lately. They replied that they had not seen him since he was supposed to have travelled to Maridi. The police then searched the house thoroughly but did not find anything. They then went to Ezboni's sister-in-law Damari's house and searched it thoroughly too. But again, they did not find anything. Thereafter, they left for Lanyi and proceeded to Piri Dri, Ezboni's home.

At the sound of approaching vehicle, Ezboni climbed one of the mango trees and was hidden by the thick foliage. The police arrived and enquired as to whether the brothers and sisters had seen Ezboni, they replied in the negative, adding that the last time they had seen him was when some police came and picked him up. Then the police searched Ezboni's house turning everything in topsy turvy and they broke several of his boxes. In one of the boxes, they found in Ezboni's handwriting the draft manifesto in which Ezboni had written and which stated that force would be used to achieve federation, if peaceful means failed. They also found draft copies of the letters which Ezboni had written to Lotada, Ali Gbatala and Taffeng and took them away. The next day, the police traveled to Lakama'di to the homestead of Ezboni's father-in-law but they did not find him there too. Now armed with incriminating documents and knowing that Ezboni was still in Moru land, they erected road blocks along all the main roads, especially on the road going to Juba.

Regarding those incriminating documents, McCall had these to say *"It is difficult to understand why and how Ezboni, a very security conscious person kept those documents in his own hand writing "*, so as to be found. Perhaps he thought that his home at Piri Dri was far in the bush and thus out of the reach of the police. Be that it may, he possibly was keeping the documents for posterity.

Re-Arrest

After a few days, Ezboni came to Lanyi and found a commercial vehicle whose owner agreed to take him to Juba. But after travelling for only a few miles, they ran into a police road block at Gori Gye'de. Ezboni was identified, arrested, hand-cuffed and taken to Maridi. Now with Ezboni in their hands and sufficient evidence to indict him, they embarked on rounding up his associates. Morris Ägyili was arrested in Mundri and was sent to Maridi. In Juba, his associates Eliaba Alau, Eliaba Ginaba and university student Noel Warille were also arrested and interrogated and later discharged; and in Khartoum, Darius Beshir was arrested, his house searched and later he also was discharged.

The Trial and Imprisonment

In Maridi, Ezboni, and Morris were charged with sedition and were transferred to Juba for trial. On 31 March 1959, Ezboni and Morris were found guilty of sedition by the Judge of the High Court. Ezboni was sentenced for nine years in prison and was transferred to Ed Damer prison to serve his term. Morris was sentenced for four years' imprisonment and was sent to serve his term in Juba prison as per his wish. He however, later was transferred to Yei prison at his request. That imprisonment fulfilled the plan of the Northerners to remove Ezboni from the political scene; particularly to prevent him from entering the Parliament, where he could have been a formidable leader for the Southern demand for federation.

As had been alluded to before, several reasons can be imputed as to why the Northerners wanted Ezboni out of the way. Firstly, though the Liberal Party was also asking for federation, the Northerners did not fear them, since they were calling for it without putting down concretely as to how it would work. But they had reason to fear Ezboni's Federal Party, because it spelt out exactly what the system would be. Secondly, they were afraid of Ezboni's strong advocacy for Southern interests and independence, his rejection of the big brother role which the Northerners were assuming and of his charismatic and strong leadership qualities. Many of them were aware of those qualities of Ezboni, since his student days in the University of Khartoum. Thirdly, they were concerned about the growing stature and influence of Ezboni and the Federal Party among the Southerners, and especially among the intellectuals. All these added together made them to conclude that Ezboni was a dangerous person and had to be denied any chance of coming to a leadership position.

With Ezboni in jail, Darius Beshir and Zakaria Yugusuk carried the ideas of Ezboni. They were continuously harassed by security and were constantly required to report to the police for interrogation. As there were no evidences against them the surveillance placed on them was later dropped.

CHAPTER IV:
POLITICAL DEVELOPMENTS WHILE EZBONI WAS IN JAIL

1958 Constituent Assembly

Composition of the 1958 Constituent Assembly

While Ezboni was serving the jail term in Ed Damer Prison, the Constituent Assembly in which he would have been a member was opened in April 1958. Its composition was such that the Umma Party (Ansar) won a narrow majority of the seats. So, in order to form a government, it was compelled to form a coalition government with the Peoples' Democratic Party (Khatmiya). The NUP, led by Ismail El Azhari, won a sizeable number of members and formed the opposition. In the South, victory went to the pro-federation Liberal Party candidates. The bitter feelings engendered by the harsh reprisals of the government in quelling the 1955 Uprising worked in favor of the pro- federalist candidates. This time around, the Southern members of

Parliament were a better educated lot, such as Fr. Saturnino Ohure of Torit, Luigi Adwok, Joseph Oduho, Elia Lupe, Franco Wil, Fr. Paul Doggale and many more. Also, this time round, the Southern ofcials and students in Khartoum organized to meet them at the airport, lest they are grabbed by Northern politicians and bought. Interestingly enough, representatives of the Northern political parties, as usual, were also there waiting for them but this time around, they failed to get them.

The Struggle for Federation in the Constituent Assembly

The sitting of the Parliament began in May 1958. The first item on the agenda was the approval of the Draft Permanent Constitution which was left over by the previous parliament. Ezboni was not there but his colleagues put up a brave fight for federation. In anticipation of the battle that was going to arise over the Draft Permanent Constitution, the Southern Members of Parliament organized themselves into a Block, under the leadership of Fr. Saturnino Ohure. The first order of business was the formation of the Constitutional Committee. Here the Southern members were disappointed when, out 43 members of the Committee, only two were Southern members. They complained about the poor representation in this critical Committee but to no avail. So, they boycotted the sittings of the Constitutional Committee and its work was paralyzed. Secondly, in June, they tabled their demand for a federal system for the Sudan to the government and which included among others: equal status for Christianity and Islam as well as equal status for English and Arabic; and an army composed only of Southerners in the South. The Assembly rejected those demands at face value, as voiced by the infamous words of Foreign Minister Ahmed Mahgoub that *"federation was given a full consideration and it was found to be unsuitable to the Sudan"*. The question was who did?

On hearing this, Southern MPs of the Block walked out and were determined not to participate in it, if federation was not included in the Draft Constitution. Interestingly, it was not only the Southerners who were objecting to the Draft Constitution, but other groups in the North as well. In a last-ditch effort, in June, Southern Block returned to the Assembly to explain their position. In that session, Fr. Saturnino made a powerful statement on the benefit of federation to the whole Sudan. Fr. Sturnino's statement provoked the interest of the marginalized groups in the North, notably, the Nuba and the Darfurians. This alarmed the Northern establishment, as it would appear to them that the idea of federation was now infecting groups in the North. In the face of this development, Prime Minister Abdullah Bey Khalil found himself in a problem. That is, disagreement with their coalition partners, the PDP; pressure from the opposition NUP; and another pressure from the Southern Block over federation. Hence, partly to debate those difficulties, but particularly to undercut the firm stand of the Southern members, the Assembly was called to a recess. Also, at about this time, the Electoral Body declared Ezboni's seat vacant and embarked on organizing a by-election in Constituency No. 4 before the end of the year.

Prelude to Military Takeover

During that time, however, there was a serious economic downturn in the country and the Northern political parties were seriously engaged in factionalism, rivalries and intrigues. The unworkable coalition between the Umma and the PDP and led by Prime Minister Abdalla Bey Khalil came under a severe stress, with Azhari's NUP playing a double game in it. Nonetheless, despite their disagreement, the Northern parties were united in their rejection of federalism.

When the Assembly reopened on 10 November, and the Southern members noticed that federation was not going to be discussed, they walked out of the Assembly. The Northern parties tried to coax and bribe the members to forgo the demand and end their boycott, but Southern members, under the leadership of Fr. Saturnino, held firm.

On noticing that the stand of the Southern Block was unflinching, the PM and the coalition government agreed to put the two burning issues of federation and Islamic constitution on the table to be discussed on 17 November 1959. However, at this point, the coalition government of PM Abdalla Bey Khalil was in a very weak and critical situation. He made a desperate attempt in a private meeting to bring the Southern MPs to some compromise on the issue of federation but the attempt failed. Hence, in the face of the resolute Southern boycott of the Assembly because of the issue of federation, the unprecedented squabbles amongst the Northern political parties and coupled with his own fear of being marginalized, he tacitly handed over the Government to the military.

Thus on 17 November 1959, the very day scheduled for the discussion of federation, General Ibrahim Abboud, the head of the army, took over the Government in a bloodless coup. So, the by-election, which the Election Commission was arranging to be conducted in Constituency No. 4 (Mundri) to replace Ezboni, became redundant. Abboud's takeover of the Government was the first military coup in the Sudan. General Abboud prorogued the Parliament, dissolved the political parties, forbade their activities, limited the freedom of speech and dissolved all party and independent press. Meanwhile, Ezboni continued to serve his jail term in Ed Damer prison.

The Abboud Military Takeover and Suppression
Suppression, Arabization and Islamization

When General Abboud took over the government, Ezboni was in prison. The takeover was marked by political repression in the country, particularly in Southern Sudan, where it was harsher. It was immediately clear that the new Military Government was as much anti- federation as the previous Government. In the pursuit of this, the Government unleashed hordes of informers to report on what the Southerners were saying, especially as regards the topic of federation. This reached to an extent that, the mere mention of the word 'federation' was enough to make one to be arrested. In addition to this, Abboud's Government embarked on a program of Arabization and Islamization in the hope that they would bring unity. And just after a couple of months following the takeover, in early 1960, Abboud changed the rest day in Southern Sudan from Sunday to Friday, to conform to the rest day in the rest of the country. The language of instruction in schools was changed to Arabic and the use of the local languages in the bush schools was scrapped. Mosques were built in several places, even in places where there were no Muslims; *khalwas* were also established in several places all over Southern Sudan; and many chiefs were compelled to change to Islam by the Northern District Commissioners.

Thus, the situation in the South became gloomy; and although most Southerners resented the new actions of the Government, they were powerless to do anything about them. The exception were the students and pupils of secondary and intermediate schools who refused to go to classes on Sundays. Their resistance was however crushed and each of them had to be caned in order to be accepted back to the class. Additionally, three of them, finalists in Rumbek Secondary School, Edward Nyiel, John Tongun and Mathew Obur were jailed for distribution of leaflets, requesting the Southern officials to refuse to go to work on Sundays.

Formation of the Southern Resistance Movement
Underground Contacts and the Escape of the Pioneers

Another big occurrence while Ezboni was serving his jail term in Ed Damer was that, some of his colleagues who were in the Assembly continued to be active in politics and meet clandestinely. They formed an underground group in Equatoria. The group comprised of the ex- MPs, political activists, government officials and other intellectuals. With the repression having reached unprecedented levels, the group concluded that some of them must go outside to voice the suffering of the people to the world. Thus, as narrated in Severino Fuli's book, in December 1960 and under the pretext of going to spend the Christmas in the house of Joseph Oduho the Headmaster of Palotaka Intermediate School, the following politicians gathered in his Oduho's house on 24 December: Fr. Satrurnino Ohure, Ferdinand Adyang, Marko Rume, Aggrey Jaden, Pankrazio Ochieng, Nathaniel Oyet, Alexis Mbale (from Wau) and of course Joseph Oduho. On the night of 24 December, they fled to Kitgum in Uganda. Those were the <u>pioneers</u> of the Southern Resistance Movement, which eventually resulted in the independence of South Sudan in July 2011. A month later, in January 1961, William Deng Nhial, a Dinka from Tonj and an Assistant District Commissioner at Kapoeta, joined the eight pioneers in Kitgum.

Formation of the Political Wing:
Sudan Africa Closed District National Union (SACDNU)

In order to voice and articulate the suffering of the people of Southern Sudan, the pioneer politicians formed a political organization called Sudan Africa Closed District National Union, with Oduho as President and William Deng as Secretary General. (NB: The Closed Districts of the Sudan was created by the Condominium Government and which carved out areas of indigenous non-Arabized Africans that included Southern Sudan, Nuba Mountains, Ingessana of Southern Blue Nile Province and parts of Darfur). It was called so because the pioneers had hoped that, the party would include all those African groups in the North. However, after sometime, they decided to shorten the name to Sudan African National Union.

The party had three key persons: Fr. Saturnino as Patron and held the purse strings; Joseph Oduho as President; and William Deng Nhial as the Secretary General. The three made extensive tours in Africa, Europe and the US to publicize the plight of the people of Southern Sudan. However, as a reaction to this, the Government promulgated the Missionary Act of 1962 to control the activities of the missionaries and the Church, because the

Government believed that it was the missionaries who were supporting the group outside. Later in 1964, when the 1962 Act did not stop the growing rebellion, the Government expelled the foreign missionaries from Southern Sudan. As reaction to this publicity, the Government of the Sudan intensified the repression in Southern Sudan, targeting those whom it believed were collaborators or sympathizers of the Movement outside.

Formation of the Military Wing (The Anyanya)

As had been mentioned before, several ex-Torit soldiers hold outs like Second Liutenant Taffeng Lodongi began to be associated with the Movement as the beginning of the fighting force, precursor to Anyanya. In April 1963, First Lt. Joseph Lagu defected from the Sudan Army and joined the military wing of the Movement. Lagu's joining gave a boost of military professionalism to the fighting force. On 30 July of the same year, SANU President Oduho called a meeting to give a meaningful name to the fighting group. From among several suggestions, the meeting, comprising of Oduho, Lagu and Fuli accepted the word ANYANYA,[5] a Ma'di word suggested by Fuli and meaning snake poison, was adopted. President Oduho then appointed Joseph Lagu to be in charge of the force under the title of officer for Special Forces.

The prime Anyanya manifesto was to "*To wage strenuous war against Arab imperialism for complete independence of Southern Sudan*" Soon after this, President Oduho was arrested

---

5   There is a controversy as to the origin of the word. Whereas it is generally accepted as a Ma'di word, there are views that say that the word is of common use by many tribes in Eastern Equatoria

by the Uganda Government for organizing military operations against the Sudan. However, despite the jailing of Oduho, the Anyanya began to be formed spontaneously in many localities all over the South. Unfortunately, most of them were formed by individuals of varied backgrounds and low level of education; and almost all of them were formed on tribal basis. All these factors came to haunt the Movement in later years.

As was the case everywhere in Southern Sudan, the Anyanya Movement came to be formed in Moru land in 1963. One group was sent by General Joseph Lagu and the other by an independent minded person Jackson Garaŋwa, known as Jeke. The two groups would not see eye to eye and as will be told later, their differences impacted heavily on Ezboni's political career. Because of that, the story of the Moru Anyanya will be dealt with in more details in Chapter VI.

CHAPTER V:
RELEASE FROM JAIL, FALL OF ABBOUD AND BACK TO POLITICS

Release and a Teaching Job and Encounter with Joseph Lagu

While the Southern Resistance Movement (SACDNU and SANU) and its military wing Anyanya were being formed in Uganda, Ezboni was still in jail in Ed Damer. In June 1962, he completed his jail term and came to Khartoum. It is noteworthy to mention here that, by this time, his assistant Morris had already completed his jail term earlier in March 1961. Ezboni's immediate plan was to proceed home to Southern Sudan, but in view of the active anti-Sudan resistance group in Uganda, the Abboud Government was afraid that he might join that group and so they refused to allow him to go home. Instead, they gave him a teaching job in the new Girls' Secondary School at Kassala. So, Ezboni went to Kassala and began to teach there.

During the school holidays in March 1963, he was allowed to go to the South. Coincidently, the boat on which he was traveling was also carrying First Lt Joseph Lagu, who was going for home leave. This leave turned out to be his last leave from the Sudan Army. As I was also on that boat, I had the chance to witness a frosty encounter between the two of them. While Lagu was genuinely enthusiastic to see Ezboni, the Southern nationalist, Ezboni did not open up to him, most probably because Lagu was a military person and Ezboni had grown not to trust persons in uniform. Very much embarrassed, I recall Lagu muttering words to the effect that Ezboni will know who he really was, that is, a Southern nationalist too. As it happened, Lagu went home to Nimule and joined the fighting group that was being organized by SANU. He did not go back to the Sudan army while Ezboni returned to Kassala after completing his leave.

The Fall of Abboud's Military Regime and Ezboni's Return to Politics
Anyanya Embarks on Activities

The fall of Abboud' military regime can be traced directly to the activities of the Anyanya. By August-September 1963, the leadership of the Movement both political (Fr Saturnino) and military (Joseph Lagu) moved to Congo to launch military activities. At the same time, the Anyanya Movement began to spread to many parts of Southern Sudan and they began to launch attacks on Government units, police and army posts. Also, during this period, many people, students, officials and ordinary citizens, began to run away to join the Movement. What however led to the fall of Abboud's military regime was that in October 1964, a group of Anyanya attacked the school at Kwajena, some few miles east of Wau and they killed six Northern teachers. The news was suppressed by the Government but later, when it became known, the people in the North were angry. They however, were unable to do anything about it. However, this news, together with several previous ones, prompted the students of the University of Khartoum to hold a rally in the Student Union premises to discuss this issue, together with the political repression which the Abboud Government was practicing. The Government, however, did not want the rally to take place. They were afraid that politicians from outside would use the rally to attack the Government.

So, on the day of the rally 21 October 1964, they sent a platoon of policemen to the University to stop the students from holding the rally, but the students refused to give up on their program; and in the ensuing melee between the police and the students, two students Ghorashi and Babiker were shot dead by the police. The death of the students, coupled with the suppression of freedoms provoked a full riot in Khartoum against Abboud's Regime.

The Fall of General Abboud

After some couple of days of riots, the dormant trade unions and professional associations, sprang to action and called for a general strike. All institutions were closed, except for those handling essential services of water, electricity and hospital and so Government work grounded to a halt. As those were going on, the professional associations handed a petition to General Abboud asking him to step down. A National Front, comprising the professional associations and the political parties, was formed to negotiate the handing of powers to the civilians. After some negotiations, Abboud agreed to step down but on condition that he would not be tried. In the meantime, while Abboud was negotiating with the National Front, his ministers were placed under house arrest. Abboud, however, remained in power to give the National Front and the political parties enough time to form a government. While this was going on, the Southerners in Khartoum also formed a front of their own called 'Southern Front' that would serve as a vehicle for their participation in the negotiations for the change of government as well as look after the interest of the Southerners in the new dispensation.

The Transitional Government, Ezboni Becomes a Minister by Southern Demand

The National Front agreed to form a transitional government for six months to be headed by neutral professionals, and assigned two ministerial positions to the Southerners. The National Front then settled on Sir El Khatim El Khalifa, former Assistant Director of Education for Southern Provinces, to be the Prime Minister for the transitional government. Then the Southerners, now firmly behind the Southern Front, made it known to the National Front that, this time around, they would choose their own representatives in the Government. Furthermore, they demanded that they would not want to be given lowly ministries, such as of animal resources again.

The Southern Front objective was to select strong,

well- educated and nationalistic representatives, who could bravely present Southern views and interests in and to the Government in general and the Northerners in particular. After a search their choice fell to Ezboni and Clement Mboro, both of whose political stand and views *vis a vis* the North were well-known to most Southerners. Hence, Southern Front submitted the names of Clement Mboro and Ezboni Gwonza for appointment as ministers in the transitional government. But when the names of the ministers came to be announced on the radio, Clement's name was announced as Minister of Interior; but instead of Ezboni, the name of Ambrose Wol, who was not nominated by Southern Front, was announced as the second Southern Minister for Communications and Transport. Upon hearing this, Southern Front and all the Southerners were furious about the change. Southern Front immediately demanded the removal of Ambrose's name and reinstating of Ezboni's name. They warned that failing that, they would not participate in the transitional government. The Northerners relented and cancelled the name of Ambrose Wol and Ezboni's name was reinstated. As is easily clear, this incident underscored the Northern dislike for Ezboni.

Thus, with his name reinstated, Ezboni came from Kassala to Khartoum to take up the position of Minister of Communications and Transport. It is to be mentioned here that since independence, that was the first time that Southerners ever occupied important Ministries such as for Interior and Communications and Transport. Usually, they were assigned some insignicant ministries like that of animal resources.

For Ezboni, this was the first time for him to work in the government. He therefore was determined to make an impact and so he took up the assignment with gusto. In a very short time, the officials of the Ministry found out that he was decisive and straight forward. Nothing was pending on his table and he demanded that the executives do likewise. He was always the first to come to office and was also the last to leave office. In the post-revolution period, several officers in all ministries were being purged for collaboration with the defunct junta. Ezboni did not act so, after all he did not know the executives well enough. But when the door of the aircraft that was taking the ex-junta detainees to Zalingei opened just after takeoff, Ezboni promptly purged the Director General of Sudan Airways, a Mr. Abdel Bagi,

The December 6th Incident in Khartoum
The Southern Riots

After a couple of months, though the military regime had fallen, and the political prisoners in the North had been released but in the South, the Northern administrators and the military were still behaving and mistreating the people as if nothing had happened. Consequently, sometime towards the end of November, Clement Mboro, the Minister of Interior and prominent member of Southern Front, was dispatched to the South by the Cabinet in order to assure people that the repression by the defunct military regime was over and that the people should go back to live their normal lives. He particularly went to some districts, like Kodok, where some Northern District Commissioners were still holding political detainees in prison. After the visit, he was scheduled to return to Khartoum on Sunday, 06 December.

On that day, Southern Front mobilized the Southerners in

Khartoum to go to the airport to give Clement a rousing reception. The plane was scheduled to takeoff from Malakal, and to arrive at Khartoum by the afternoon. Hence, many Southerners went to the airport to meet him. But the plane delayed and did not arrive at the scheduled time. The people began to complain and murmur and soon they became agitated. Given the high mistrust of Northerners and since no reason was given for the delay, they began to imagine that, either the Northerners had done something sinister to Clement in the South or were deliberately delaying the plane, so that they would not accord him the rousing reception they had planned for him.

By six o'clock, their anger broke out in the open. They began to break windows in the airport and came to the street (Sharia Ifrikiya) and began to stone any passing vehicles. As they dispersed and on their way home, they continued with the same riotous activities. When they reached Khartoum center, they ran into Northern Sudanese crowds coming out of a football match and the cinemas. Annoyed at the destruction being wreaked by the Southerners, they reacted and started to beat up any Southerner. Thus being out-numbered by the Northern Sudanese crowds, many Southerners were beaten up and even some were killed.

The beating up and killing of Southerners spread to other parts of the town. The situation was as follows: there were serious attacks on Southerners in Khartoum Center, Burri, Khartoum North, Shambat and Kober. In the Deims, there were some few attacks on Southerners that night but they ceased the following day. There, however, were no retaliatory attacks of Southerners in the whole of Omdurman and El Shaggara. In those other areas of the city, the attack on Southerners continued for the next two to three days. Interestingly, while that was going on, the police, who were all Northerners, did nothing to stop it. Yes, the Southerners misbehaved by destroying property, beating up and even killing a few Northerners. So, the initial reaction of the Northerners was understandable, but for the police to allow Southerners to be hunted, injured or killed for subsequent three days, it was irresponsible on their part. As this went on, the international community in Khartoum became alarmed by the inaction of the Government. So, in reaction to this concern, the Government belatedly took action. Thus, the police went round the residential areas to collect trapped and frightened Southerners in their houses. They were taken to the football stadia of Khartoum and Mourada. In view of this, the Southern students in the University of Khartoum, the writer included, had to forgo their studies in order to distribute food to the displaced people in the football stadia.

Ezboni's Lone Action

As the situation began to improve, many Southerners in the stadia were afraid to go back and live in their houses in the residential areas. Many now longed to return to Southern Sudan but they did not have the means for transporting themselves and their plight reached Ezboni. Consequently, Ezboni, as the Minister for Transport, singlehandedly (without cabinet approval) gave instructions to the Sudan Railways to allow any frightened Southerner to board the week's south-bound train and/or steamer to go south free of charge. Hence, the week's train and steamer to Malakal-Juba as well as the train to Wau were full of frightened Southerners who were eager to return to Southern Sudan and to go free of charge.

This action by Ezboni annoyed the Northerners in the Government, the Northern public and the press. Ezboni was roundly condemned for effecting such an action without cabinet approval and they began to accuse him of implementing his objective of separation by transporting Southerners back home. For that reason, many of them demanded that Ezboni should be removed from the cabinet but Southern Front rejected this. In contrast, this action earned him accolades and the admiration of all the Southerners. He was now seen as one who had the courage to stand in front of the Northerners for their sake and particularly it earned him the gratitude of those who grasped the chance to return home. Thus, he became well-known all over the Southern Sudan as a courageous Southern nationalist, who would stand by his people. To the Northerners, however, this incident was a confirmation of their long- standing view of Ezboni as a dangerous separatist. Thus, their problem now became how to remove Ezboni from the scene.

William Deng's Proposal and Return to Sudan

But while all that was happening in Khartoum, earlier in October and immediately after the fall of Abboud's military regime, William Deng wrote a letter to the Transitional Government from his base in Congo[6] expressing SANU's willingness to return to the Sudan to negotiate a solution to the Southern problem. He did that without information to his colleagues in Uganda. That proposal was welcome by Prime Minister Sir El

---

6   Because of a disagreement between him (Secretary General) and Joseph Oduho (President), William Deng relocated from Kampala to reside in Congo.

Khatim and the Northern establishment and a proposal for a round table conference was put forward. However, in Kampala, his colleagues and Aggrey Jaden, the new SANU President,[7] were angry with him for unilaterally writing to Khartoum and in the name of SANU.

In early January 1965, William Deng arrived at Kampala on his way to the Sudan. His colleagues in Kampala attempted to dissuade him from going to Khartoum on the grounds that the best way for Southern Sudan was SANU to stay outside to continue the struggle, but he refused. Additionally, the Southern Front in Khartoum also tried to dissuade him by pleading to him that, it would be better if he could wait a little so that he could come together for the conference with his colleagues as one SANU. They underscored to him that, coming together would demonstrate unity in the Movement in the eyes of the Northerners and the world. But William would not accept those arguments and insisted on going back to the Sudan. Thus, on 27 February 1965, he left for Khartoum with a group of non-entities in the Movement and was received by the Northerners only. Southern Front and the majority of Southerners in Khartoum boycotted his arrival. At his arrival, he stated in the radio that he represented the true SANU. That statement upset his other colleagues in Kampala to no end.

---

7   From 7-14 October 1964, the rst SANU National Convention was held and Aggrey Jaden was elected the President of SANU, replacing Joseph Oduho. At this time William Deng was also no more a Secretary General of SANU.

The Round Table Conference

In the meantime, pressure for a conference between the South and North for finding a solution to the war was growing; even Southern Front accepted the holding of the conference. However, SANU outside with Aggrey was not very ready for it and were concerned about where the venue of the conference would be. When they finally got to accept the holding of the conference, they proposed that it should be held outside the Sudan. But the Government and the Northern parties insisted on holding it in Khartoum. Thus the venue for the conference became a problem. To resolve it, the Government sent a two-man delegation of Abdin Ismail and Ezboni Mondiri to Kampala to persuade SANU (Aggrey) to accept to come to Khartoum for the conference but the delegation failed to convince them. Their attitude had hardened because William Deng, who was already in Khartoum, was claiming that he represented SANU. In view of this stalemate, the Government and Northerners were began to consider holding the conference without SANU of Aggrey. But since that would not be good to the Southern position, Southern Front sent a delegation headed by Hilary Logali and comprising of Darius Beshir and Daniel Jumi. This delegation was able to convince SANU led by Aggrey to come to Khartoum for the conference

*Preparations for the Conference
and the Telephone Exchange Incident*

When it was certain now that SANU Aggrey would attend the Conference, Southern Front began to prepare for it. It formed several committees and sought views from the Southern Front branch offices in Juba, Wau and Malakal. As the Minister of Transport and Communication, Ezboni was tasked to keep in touch with those Southern Front branches in the South and to bring their delegations to attend the Conference in Khartoum. One night at around midnight, Ezboni wanted to speak by telephone to the head of the delegation at Wau. So, from his house, he called the telephone exchange to give him the line to Wau. But the phone rang and rang and there was no response. Having tried again and again without success, Ezboni decided to drive to the telephone exchange. When he went into the exchange room, he found that the official who should have given him the line was fast asleep. Ezboni was angry. According to him, he pulled the official from his sleep and shook him, possibly violently, but did not slap him. The following day, the Ministry and town were abuzz with the story that Ezboni had slapped a telephone operator at the place of work. Be that it may, it was wrong for Ezboni to have physically handled or slapped the worker at the place of work.

This story was music to the ears of the Northerners who, in the rst place, did not like Ezboni in the cabinet; and this incident provided them with a golden opportunity to eject him from it. They therefore requested Southern Front to withdraw Ezboni out of the cabinet and send a replacement but Southern Front was reluctant to act on that request, particularly at that time when the Round Table Conference was just about to be held. In view of that, they delayed their response pending the conclusion of the Conference.

Ezboni Resigns from the Cabinet

After the Conference, the Northerners renewed their request to Southern Front to withdraw Ezboni from the cabinet but Southern Front refused. So, to force their demand, they induced all the employees of the Ministry of Transport and Communication to go on strike and they followed that with the threat that, if Ezboni was not removed, then the larger General Sudan Workers Trade Union could go on strike in support of the workers of the Ministry of Transport and Communications. So in order to save Southern Front from the embarrassment of withdrawing him, Ezboni himself tendered his resignation and Southern Front nominated Gordon Mourtat to replace him in the Cabinet.

Departure for the South and Home

As soon as Ezboni was relieved, he got on the first available train and steamer to go home to the South. By the time the authorities came to know of his whereabouts, he had already left and was already on the steamer and was approaching Juba. To them, Ezboni should not have been allowed to leave Khartoum for fear that he would join and reinforce the Anyanya, if he ever got to the South. The plan therefore was to detain him in Juba so that he could not make any contacts with the Anyanya or to join them. But Ezboni, anticipating such an eventuality, decided to leave Juba promptly for the country side upon landing in Juba. He therefore arranged for a vehicle to wait for him at the river bank and to take him straight away to the country side; and that was exactly what happened. He did not even stop to go to Kator to see his wife or to greet his relatives in Juba. So, by the time the security came to the river bank, they were told Ezboni had left in a car. They then went to his wife's and relatives' homes but did not find him either. Ezboni was already gone out of the reach of the security. In Khartoum, several papers blamed the Government for allowing him to leave Khartoum because they knew he certainly would join and consequently strengthen the Southern Resistance Movement and the Anyanya, and which he certainly did.

Deliberations of the Round Table Conference

At this juncture, it may be appropriate to go back and say something about the outcome of the Round Table Conference. The Conference was duly held on 16 March 1965, while Ezboni was still a Minister but for all purposes he was going to leave the cabinet. On the side of the North, the participants in the Conference were Umma Party, Democratic Unionist Party, National Unionist Party, Islamic Charter Front, the Communist Party and the National Front. On the side of the South the participants were SANU Aggrey Jaden's wing, SANU William Deng's wing, Liberal Party, Unity Party of Santino Deng and Southern Front. Several countries sent representatives to it as observers, including Tanzania, Nigeria, Egypt and Uganda.

In the Conference, the views expressed were varied. The Northern parties wanted a united Sudan with some form of regionalism for the three Southern Provinces. William Deng's SANU wanted federation. Aggrey Jaden's SANU wanted separation of the South from the North. Southern Front called for self-determination for Southern Sudan. With such varied views, it was difficult to come up with a solution in so short a time. So, it was agreed to set up a Twelve-Man Committee of six representatives from the Southern parties and six from the Northern parties to continue the discussions within a framework. On the Southern side, the six members were two each from Southern Front, SANU William Deng and SANU Aggrey Jaden. The government was to allow representative of SANU led by Aggrey Jaden to come to attend the Committee's meetings in Khartoum. However, after the elected government of PM Mahgoub took over, the Northerners refused to give entrance visa to the SANU Aggrey's representative to attend the meetings. Additionally, the new elected government of PM Ahmed Mahgoub, adopted a bellicose attitude towards the SANU of Aggrey, the Anyanya and Southern Front and fighting resumed in full. The Twelve-Man Committee continued without SANU Aggrey but was killed by Saddig El Mahdi when he took over as Prime Minister of the country. Thus, a chance for finding a solution to the Southern problem, through the Round Table Conference was lost.

CHAPTER VI:
IN THE SOUTHERN
RESISTANCE MOVEMENT

In the previous Chapter V, we read that Ezboni promptly departed Juba for the country side after disembarking from the steamer. Here, it can be said that he was at the precipice of entering the world of the Southern Resistance Movement, the political (SANU/ALF) and its military wing the Anyanya. In his own words, the two years he spent in that world became some of the most challenging to him in his entire personal and political life. In order for us to appreciate the difficulties which he faced and roles he played in the resistance movement, we need to know something about the situation in the Southern Resistance Movement after the Round Table Conference and about the Moru Anyanya, which served as the *entre port* through which he entered into the Southern Resistance Movement.

The Southern Resistance Movement After the Round Table Conference

Disagreements and the Emergence of Azania Liberation Front (ALF)

On the political side, the situation was as follows. After the delegation that went for the Round Table Conference returned to Kampala, the relationship between Aggrey and Oduho soured. In fact, ever since he lost to Aggrey in the First Convention in September 1964, Oduho had been sulking over his loss in the elections for the presidency. He also had been critical of the Round Table Conference and his criticism increased when the Northern political parties refused to accept the representative of Aggrey's SANU to participate in the Twelve-Man Committee. And worst still, according to Fuli, Aggrey was not the favorite of the Patron, Fr. Saturnino, who held the purse strings. Additionally, there was the problem with the name of SANU, which Oduho, Aggrey and many other members did not like to share with William Deng's SANU, now inside the Sudan. Hence, Aggrey's Executive Council voted to drop the name SANU and changed the party's name to Sudan African Liberation Front (SALF). Oduho however set up a separate office and continued to use the name SANU.

In May 1965, a Southern Front delegation came to Kampala and tried to patch up the difference so that Oduho could accept Aggrey as President of the Movement, since he was elected by the Convention, but Oduho refused. The only agreement was for the change of name to SALF. Deprived of funds from the Patron, Aggrey's leadership became weak and in view of this weakness, Oduho made his move and took up the leadership of the Movement. So, in January 1966, he announced the merger of Aggrey's SALF and his SANU into the Azania Liberation Movement (ALM), later changed to Azania Liberation Front (ALF); and he declared himself as the President of the new party with its headquarters inside the Sudan at Dito in Latuka land.

This was in contrast to previous cases, where the movement operated from Uganda. At this point, Aggrey disappeared from the scene. In March 1967, as the undisputed leader, President Oduho then called for a big meeting in his home base at Dito in order to form his government as well as to chart the way forward. As we shall see later, it was in this meeting that Ezboni suddenly appeared and was instantly made Secretary for Defence of the ALF.

On the military side, the situation after the Round Table Conference was as follows. By June 1965, the ceasefire that had been agreed upon in order to create conducive atmosphere for the Round Table Conference had broken down, especially after the expiry of the term of Sir El Khatim's transitional government. The elected of Prime Minister Ahmed Mahgoub opted for a military solution and he gave a free hand to the army in the South to do anything to crush the Anyanya and the Southern Front. Given this leeway, the army undertook massacres in Juba, Wau, Warajwok, Bor, Lui (on 20 June) and many other places. Though poorly equipped and out-gunned, the Anyanya fought back and cut communication between the towns. Hence, there were no movements between towns, except under heavy military escort. Many Southerners fled the country and swelled the number of refugees as well as the ranks of Southern Resistance Movement and of the Anyanya.

The Moru Anyanya
Introduction

In the last paragraph of Chapter IV, we stated that the Moru Anyanya would be discussed in more details here because it impacted heavily on Ezboni's political career. Additionally, because it was the door through which Ezboni gained entrance into the world of the Southern Resistance Movement and it also was the theatre where he met many challenges. Hence, thoroughly understanding it would enable us to understand and appreciate the challenges which Ezboni faced. The information provided here has been gained from several sources, *viz*: from Ezboni himself; gleaned from McCall's book, then still a manuscript; from interviews with and articles from Morris Agyili, Scopas Juma; and from many other persons such as John Russie and Francis 'Bädriako. Additionally information about the Moru Anyanya, their activities and behavior were first hand observations by the writer, when he was in Moru land in the period from May to August 1965.

The Moru Anyanya, Beginnings in the Congo

The Anyanya in Moru land owes its origin to Moru political escapees in Congo. The first of these was Batilimoyo Kagyi, a government agriculturist who escaped to Congo in 1955, after the Torit Uprising. He took up a job and residence at Aba. Batilimoyo was the first and key political operative of SANU and Anyanya in Congo and was in close contact with Fr. Saturnino, Joseph Lagu, Elia Lupe, Marko Rume and others, especially when the SANU and Anyanya leadership relocated to Congo. The other person was Ezboni Jo'di, then a manager in Haggar's Tea and Tobacco Plantation at Iwatoka and who was one of the contestants in the 1958 election in Moru land on the Liberal Party ticket. He lost that election to Ezboni Gwonza. There were Clement Monyoro, one of the workers in Haggar's Tobacco Company; Repent Sunday Gideon who was a teacher and an artist with the Publications Bureau in Juba; Aggrey Ndarago Andago a nurse in Juba Hospital; and Jackson Garaŋwa, commonly called 'Jeke' by the Morus. He was a worker in the Forestry Department at Katire and he escaped to Congo, where he possibly was in contact with Ali Gbatala. Then there was Stephen Ali Baba, one of the soldiers in Ali Gbatala's (Group A) disastrous expeditionary force that was beaten back by the government army at the launch of Anyanya operations into Sudan in September 1963; and lastly there was Benjamin Tere, a student from Mundri Intermediate School. Sometime later, this group was joined by escapees from Mundri, namely, Morris Ägyili, erstwhile special assistant of Ezboni, his chief campaign manager and who was jailed with Ezboni on conviction of treason; and Ismail Rajab who, as mentioned earlier, was another of Ezboni Gwonza's close confidants and eloquent political campaigner.

Entry of Anyanya into Moru land

According to McCall, the Anyanya entered Moru land in three groups. The first probably was an unsanctioned group, led by Stephen Ali Baba and possibly Benjamin Tere. They were participants in that disastrous expedition by Group A, under Ali Gbatala into Maridi area and which was beaten back by the government forces earlier in September. They either were sent by Ali Gbatala, or decided to enter Moru land on their own. In any case, they reached in Moru land in April 1964 and established the first Anyanya camp at Rikokawa stream south of Mt Malanga near Bangolo.

The second entrance was undertaken by Jackson (Jeke) Garaŋwa, who earlier in February 1964, had gone to Faraje and met Batilimoyo and requested to be assisted to get weapons and ammunition. But Batilimoyo told him that things had changed and that it had then become difficult to purchase weapons from Congo, in view of increased restrictions by its government. Jackson therefore returned empty handed and entered into the Sudan in Bangolo area. But whether he entered earlier or before Ali Baba's group, has yet to be verified. Jackson reportedly travelled through Bangolo and northwards towards Amadi. He then went south eastwards to Kedi'ba, in his home area of the Kädiro (a Section of the Moru tribe), where he established a camp. While on his way to Kedi'ba, he recruited several pupils from the intermediate school at Mundri as well as pupils from the elementary schools at Lui and Mundri. Once established in Kedi'ba, Jackson considered his camp as coming directly under Ali Gbatala's Group A. He obstinately refused to be under Group D, which was later officially commissioned by Lagu to operate in Moru area. As will be seen later, it is this obstinate refusal to join the other Group that brought about the split in the Moru Anyanya, a split that ultimately drew Ezboni into its vortex and led to the shootout between the two groups.

As mentioned above, the third group to enter was sanctioned by Chief of Staff Joseph Lagu as Group D under El Hag Beshir, a Mondu, normally called El Hay. In its preparation to enter the Moru area Batilimoyo, who was in Faraje, requested Lagu to release Morris Ägyili from Group C to join this pioneer group to Moru land. In June 1964, the group comprising of El Hag, Morris Ägyili, Repent Sunday and later Aggrey Andago entered Moru land and proceeded to Diko area, where they set up their rst camp, along Mele stream near Angunde. According to Morris, after a few weeks, a delegation led by Benjamin Tere from Ali Baba's camp arrived at the camp to first find out who this group was; and secondly, if indeed they were Anyanya, they should come to solve a dispute between him and Ali Baba. So, El Hag requested Morris Ägyili and Repent Sunday to go and resolve that dispute, which the two succeeded to do. Thereafter, Ali Baba's group joined the main group under El Hag and sometime later, the camp in Diko area was relocated to Ä'bu in Bangolo area. In January 1965, the group decided to move its main camp (headquarters) eastwards across River Yei on River Mosa at Mayaya, south of present day Lozo. They then established a smaller camp down River Yei at a pool (täṛi) called Gori Udru for the Engineering Unit under Hitler Musa. As the case was, both of those camps were located in the area of the Miza Section of the Moru tribe. This group initially called itself Group F but in June 1965, it officially changed its denotation to an independent Groups D.[8] In the overall Anyanya military structure, however, Group D was still under Brigadier Ali Gbatala who was the Deputy to the overall Commander Major General Taffeng Lodongi. It is however, to be mentioned that until 1967, there was an ill-defined relationship between this Group and Ali Gbatala's Group A.

---

8   Note: Due to poor Anyanya command structure, there also is another Group D in the east bank.

The Split: Two Anyanya Groups

As time went on the group led by Stephen Ali Baba and Benjamin Tere joined the main group. Hence, there came to be two Anyanya groups in Moru land: Group D, known as the Mayaya Group under El Hag; and the Kedi'ba Group under Jackson Garaŋwa and who preferred to be under Ali Gbatala's Group A. In the meantime, both the Mayaya and Kedi'ba Groups embarked on massive propaganda and recruitment drives. In this, while the Mayaya Group won over more mature persons, especially the ex-Torit soldiers, the Kedi'ba Group could only win over raw school pupils and other youngsters. The relationship between the two groups however became very estranged. According to Morris Ägyili, all efforts to persuade Jackson so that the two groups could merge failed and as time went on, this difference only got worse. The Mayaya Group felt that they were the real Anyanya, because their group was formed and commissioned by the Chief of Staff Joseph Lagu to operate in Moru area, whereas the other group was not. Secondly and rightly so, they considered themselves more mature and with much more military experience than the Kedi'ba Group. They considered the Kedi'ba Group as mere upstarts or youngsters. This difference persisted until the arrival of Ezboni and as we shall see later, it eventually drew Ezboni Mondiri into vortex and it became his Achilles heel in trying to unite and reform the Moru Anyanya. It also came to have a lingering effect on his political standing and also on the local politics in Moru land.

Local Anyanya Structure

As to its structure, the local Anyanya structure was similar to the Anyanya structure elsewhere in the country. In both the Mayaya and Kedi'ba Groups, they consisted of two components: the fighters, the Anyanya proper, who carried arms and who did the fighting; and the Scouts, who carried no firearms and who mediated between the Anyanya and the civilians. The Scouts also rendered administration, undertook policing, collected food for the fighters, mobilized porters and, at times, dispensed justice.

In the Mayaya Group (Group D), the command was as follows: El Hag Yousif Beshir, the overall commander and was supported by senior officers, comprising of Morris Ägyili Kayanga, Repent Sunday Gideon and Aggrey Ndarago Andago. For its military operations, the Group divided Mundri District into two areas: east of River Yei, supposed to include the Kedi'ba area, under Yotama Bariŋwa; and the area west of River Yei, under Morris Ägyili. For the administration of civilians, there were Head Scouts who were assigned areas of responsibility. Those Head Scouts, unfortunately, were made to eclipse the authority of the traditional Chiefs, rendering the chiefs jobless, belittled and/or redundant. In the areas east of River Yei, they approximately were: Samsona Kyiriri in Singo area; Eliaza Dawidi in Lui area; Charles Gwonza in Piri/Lanyi area; Yosepata Biringi in Luŋwa area, to mention but a few. In the west bank, there were Batwele Ciniŋwa, later Edward Kọre in Bari area, Gabriel Pataki Dodo in Tore Wande area and so on. Unfortunately, the military hierarchy and administrative set up under the Kedi'ba Group was not immediately available to the writer. All efforts to obtain information about the structure of the Kedi'ba Group from Jackson Garaŋwa were unsuccessful, as he was cut off by the latest round of fighting in South Sudan.

Anyanya Treatment of Civilians

Both groups in Mayaya and Kedi'ba did not treat the civilians well and so the civilians were living in fear of the Anyanya. The fighters, who were given up to moving around for no good reason, showed absolutely no respect to elders, teachers, pastors or chiefs. In any slight disagreement with a civilian an Anyanya fighter would quickly resort to the threat in Moru: "*Odra i'dwo mi ya ya?*" literally translates to, "Do you not have death in you?" This was a way of saying "Are you not afraid of death?"

Some of the worst behavior of the Anyanya was towards those whom they alleged to be government informers. But in fact, in almost all cases, all those they accused were actually not government informers at all. Very often, one was called an informer simply for calling to question something they were doing wrongly. Many such victims would be tied with a strong thin twine; and using a method acquired from the Congolese rebels called '*mondele avion*', both the arms and legs of the victim would be tied behind, so that he/she would lie on the chest. It was the cruelest way of treating a human being. The writer was a personal witness to the case of a woman who was residing with the soldiers in Mundri. She came out of the town to collect firewood and was captured by the Anyanya sentries. It was heart wrenching and unbearable to see the cruel, inhuman torture she was subjected to. Many such falsely accused victims, and this woman included, would admit to being an informer, just from the body pain so that he/she could be finished off with.

Furthermore, the Anyanya would not ask but demand or force the people to give them what they wanted; and very often, they were engaged in the raping of girls.

Worst still, in some areas, the Anyanya were also engaged in arresting, torturing and killing of persons who were alleged to be evil doers (*kole*) or sorcerers (*mato*). Some of the worst cases of this happened in Singo area, which was witnessed and recorded by Watts Roba Gibia in his book 'The Norms, Culture and Traditions of the Moru People'. Watts writes that the local commander in Singo area rounded up several women, who were suspected to be evil doers (*kole*), tortured them and who, from body pain, admitted that they indeed were evil doers and had been responsible for the death of such and such person. In Kädiro area, the Anyanya cut off the ears of a young man called Isaac Owuṛu, just because it was alleged that he was a sorcerer (*mato*).

As a consequence, the people were cowed and so a few fled to Juba and some even fled to the army garrison in Mundri. Additionally, some of the uneducated Anyanya leaders and officers were hostile to students and were preventing the school boys and girls from going to continue their education elsewhere. That was on the grounds that it was the season for fighting and nobody should opt out.

CHAPTER VII:
EZBONI ARRIVES HOME, CHALLENGES AND EXPLOITS

Arrival Home, Disappointments

After slipping out of Juba, Ezboni arrived home in his homestead in Piri Dri in about the middle of April 1965. The homestead was about three kilometers west of Lanyi which is on the main road to Juba. At that time, his brother, Charles Gwonza, was the Head Scout for the Anyanya in the area. In reviewing his experience during the 20 months he spent at home with the Moru Anyanya, Ezboni told the writer that, that period was one of the most disappointing, frustrating and challenging periods in his entire political life. Because, he was not only misunderstood and misrepresented by his own people, but was also humiliated by them. He, however, said that he was not holding anything against any of them nor had he given up on them, because, they did not know any better; and adding that he would continue to serve them as best as his abilities would permit. He also professed to take consolation in the saying that a prophet was not always accepted in his own home.

The Situation in Moru Land at the Time of Ezboni's Arrival

At the time of his arrival, the situation in Moru land was as follows: the authority of the Government had virtually collapsed, except for the presence of some policemen at Mide (Jambo's Corner), in Mundri, Yeri and in Mvolo. The authority of the chiefs had completely been undermined by the Anyanya and so they were not anymore fulfilling their normal responsibilities of administering the people, dispensing justice and collecting poll tax. In fact, the popular Chief and ex-member of Parliament, Timon Biro Mbäriŋwa, had been assassinated by the Anyanya unit in Singo area on the grounds that he was still collecting taxes for the government. Education had ceased and more than eight schools had been burnt down by the Anyanya. On the health side, the hospital at Lui was however still functioning but most of the outlying dispensaries had closed.

Regarding the prosecution of the war, the situation Ezboni found was not very encouraging. There were no political commissars and so there were no programs of political education to tell the people as to the reasons why the Southerners were fighting, except harping on the peoples' dislike for the Northerners (Mundukuru). Moreover, there was no appeal to them to support the war effort voluntarily, except by force.

On the military front, and as explained above, Ezboni found out that the Moru Anyanya was divided into two rival groups, the Mayaya and Kedi'ba Groups. The former was larger, comprised of more experienced and mature soldiers, and was commanded by El Hag Beshir while the latter was smaller, comprising of inexperienced youngsters and was commanded by Jackson Garaŋwa (Jeke). Both groups were antagonistic to each other and both had meager weapons and ammunitions. Most of the fighters in both groups were only armed with bows, arrows, spears and machetes. Additionally, the Anyanya military structure was a very poor one; and discipline was not properly enforced. Consequently, any ordinary fighter who found himself alone anywhere was law unto himself. Furthermore, many were drinking heavily to the extent that the camps became centres of merriment and partying, where pleasure girls, often taken to the camps as prisoners, were kept busy brewing alcoholic drinks, especially the honey-based drink, *duma*.

Ezboni's Shock

The above was the situation Ezboni found in Moru land. He therefore was greatly shocked and disheartened by what he saw and heard about the behavior of the Anyanya in Moru land and especially by their mistreatment of the people. Some of the things they were doing to the civilians were quite out of the character and culture of the Moru people. Like many others, Ezboni wondered as to how this strange behavior of indescribable cruelty came to be practiced by some elements of those Moru Anyanya to their own kinsfolk. This is because, the Moru people were not known for such cruelty and especially in the taking away of human lives "*lämi ako*" (without justification). As is the case, the Moru take homicide to be a serious taboo. They believed that leprosy is the direct result of taking away of a human life, an act which not only would afflict the killer, but his descendants as well. For this reason, even when a person has killed a sworn enemy and who equally could have done the same to him, the person would have to undergo a very strict ritual cleansing process.

The preponderance of school pupils in the ranks of the Anyanya was also very disturbing to Ezboni. To him, they should have been at school learning. It therefore became clear to him that the local Anyanya had lost direction. That is, instead of doing what they took up arms for, they had turned to doing irrelevant things.

Decision to Reform the Local Anyanya

He therefore took those as personal challenges to him and decided that he must reform the organization and to put an end to those bad practices by joining the movement. He felt that by being in the organization, he would be in a better position to educate and influence them to desist from those practices and make them to have wider understanding of what the struggle was all about. Additionally, Ezboni was very disappointed with the split in the Moru Anyanya and so he thus prioritized the unity and integration of the two groups. He felt he could achieve this, given his immense standing and popularity among Southern Sudanese people in general and the Moru people in particular.

Ezboni thus joined the Anyanya, that is, the Mayaya Group, not because of any preference, or on the grounds of being a Miza but for the simple reason that they were nearest to his home. Furthermore, because his brother Charles was a Head

Scout, many Anyanya officers as well as rank and file passed through Charles' home and so Ezboni was able to interact with them. Fortunately for him, they readily accepted his words and leadership.

The Kedi'ba Incident, Addressing the First Challenge

Now almost a leader in the Moru Anyanya, Ezboni began by undertaking a tour of the local area to acquaint himself with the situation and to enlighten the Anyanya about the struggle and thereby dissuade them from such bad behavior. He visited the Lui area and while he was there at Area Commander Yotama Bariŋwa's camp, news arrived that a fight had broken out between the civilians and the Anyanya fighters at Kedi'ba and that many civilians were beaten and others tied up and houses were burnt. The writer was present when that news was brought to him. It was reported that Jackson Garaŋwa, the head of the group, was not present because he had gone to Congo.

That incident, as narrated by Francis 'Badriako Iniŋwa, an intermediate school teacher, Benedict Tarifo Gyirimani and corroborated by John Russie, a member of the Kedi'ba Anyanya was that, there was a big dance festival at Kedi'ba, in which many people, including elements of the local Anyanya, had gathered. Many of the youth, Anyanya and non-Anyanya, were however drunk. And as is the case in Moru culture, beating the big drum, *dugye*, is a prestigious act and invariably young men would like to show off their prowess in the beating. As is usually the case, there always was an intense competition among the young men to beat the *dugye*, the Anyanya included. Additionally, as is also the case, while dancing, young men would carry fires on bundles of grass. The reason for this is yet to be known. Normally, when one of them wants to get rid of the ash of the fire, he would do so by striking the ground. But reportedly some of the inebriated Anyanya fighters in that dance would instead strike the ash on some of the dancers. Given the already bad relationship between the people and the Anyanya because of mistreatment, that made the non-Anyanya young men and the people very angry and they beat them up. There then ensued a general fight between the civilians and the Anyanya fighters and the civilians over-powered them, took their guns and even burnt down their nearby small camp.

Anyanya Retaliation

When those fighters ran, and reported the matter to the main camp, on the following day, a force was sent to exact revenge for what took place. Upon arrival, they started beating up everyone, including women and children. In the beating, one called Yorama Lalume Tiga was struck in the eye and he lost that eye. Francis 'Bädriako, the intermediate school teacher, Benedict Tarifo Gyirimani, then a Rumbek Secondary School student and many others were beaten and tied up. They were brought to the chief's compound as prisoners. Furthermore, many homesteads, like that of the Kodo'ba were burnt down. This brought a hostile and a very bad relationship between the civilians and the local Anyanya. Perhaps, if the leader of the Kedi'ba Group, Jackson Garaŋwa, had been around, he probably might have stopped it.

Ezboni heard this with dismay and because he did not finish the work at Lui, he decided to send an envoy from the Mayaya Group with the message that the captives should immediately be released, adding that he would soon be visiting Kedi'ba and would not like to see any person tied up and/or in captivity. Upon receiving his message, the Anyanya did release the captives. That quick response to Ezboni's order by the Kedi'ba Anyanya indicated the degree of respect which all the Moru Anyanya had for him at that time, irrespective of the Group they belonged to. After completing the engagement at Lui, Ezboni went to Kedi'ba to make sure that the strained relationship between the civilians and the Anyanya had been resolved. He also took it as an opportunity to mediate the differences between the two groups of the Anyanya, the Kedi'ba and the Mayaya Groups.

Magnitude of the Challenges

Given the situations described above, characterized by disunity, misbehavior, indiscipline and ill-treatment of civilians by the Anyanya, Ezboni came to realize the enormous tasks the reform he had in mind would entail, if he were ever to mould the Anyanya into an effective and a disciplined fighting force to fight against the northern dominated government in Khartoum. He came to consider that the tasks comprised of: enlightening the people and the Anyanya fighters about the objectives of the struggle; reconciling the two groups of the local Anyanya; reforming and building the local Anyanya to be an effective fighting force through training and acquisition of weapons; educating the local Anyanya to have a more nationalistic outlook; to realize that theirs was just one of a whole group of Anyanya forces in Southern Sudan, fighting for a common goal; separating the military from the civilian affairs; and organizing a civil administration that would render social services and administer justice to the ordinary civilians. Ezboni felt he was up to the task, trusting in his ability which McCall described as, *"Although no soldier, Ezboni had a genius for organization and took an early hand in military operations"*

Ezboni's First Military Operation
Conceiving a Military Operation

Early in June, Ezboni visited Kedi'ba, together with some leaders of the Mayaya Group. The purpose of the visit was twofold: to cool the tense relationship between the Anyanya at Kedi'ba and the civilians; and to reconcile the difference between the Kedi'ba and Mayaya Groups. Jackson Garaŋwa was the still in Congo. In the meeting, both sides agreed to work and coordinate their military operations together. Upon return, Ezboni conceived a military operation that would be jointly executed by the two groups as a way to consummate the agreement. That operation was to be an attack on the police post at Jambo (Mide). As stated earlier, Jambo was the only remaining out post of the government outside of Mundri town. Ezboni believed that, if that joint operation was successful, the attack would not only have removed government presence in that area, but gained some weapons, vehicles and radio for the Anyanya. Additionally, it would improve the relationship between the two Groups and boost their morale. He envisaged the operation to be a joint action between the two Groups and it was as represented in the sketch shown opposite.

Sketch I: Eziboni's Battle Plan (Not to Scale)

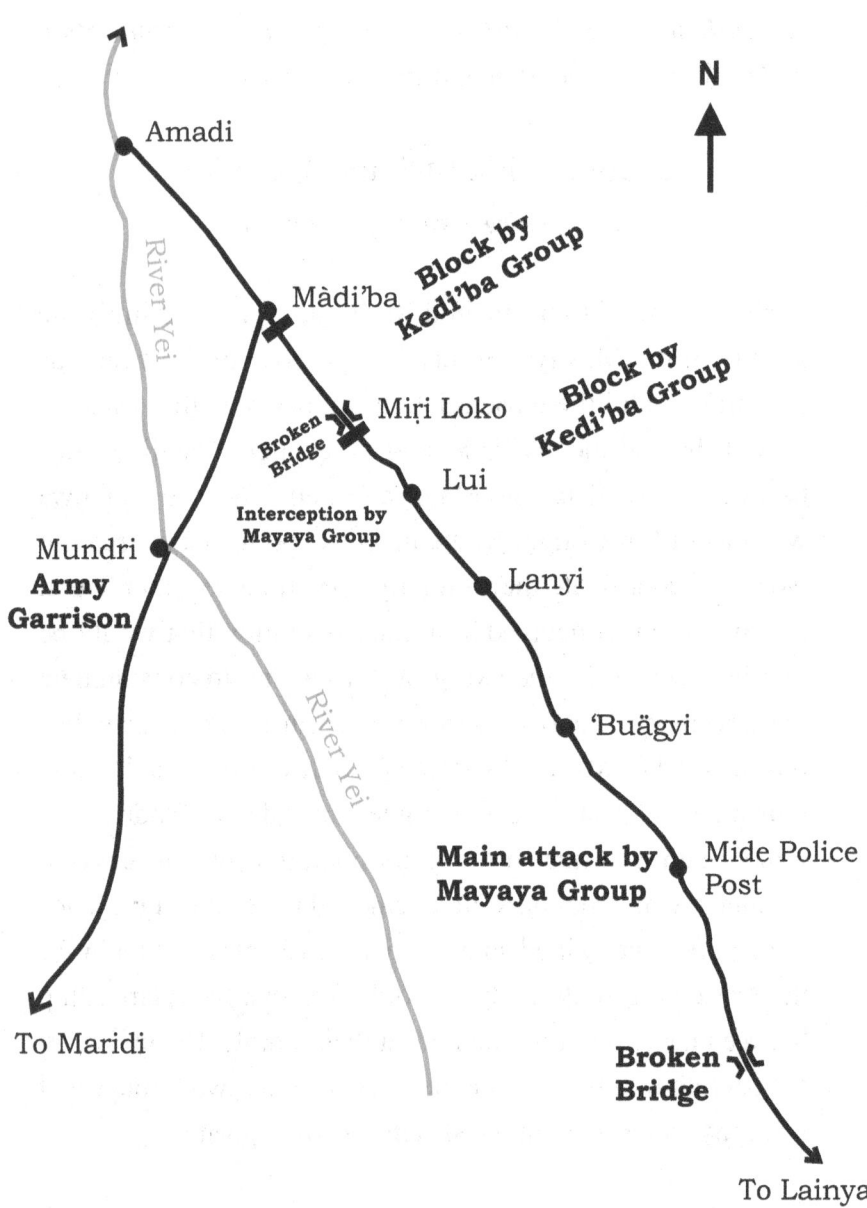

The plan was for a unit of the main Anyanya group of Mayaya to execute the attack on the police post at Mide (Jambo). But before doing so, they were to break the bridge over River Kipo to prevent the police from escaping along that road to Juba, as well as to prevent any rescue coming from that direction. Another Mayaya unit under Yotama Bariŋwa was to take position at Lui to intercept any escapees from Jambo heading to Mundri and also prevent any reinforcement that Mundri might want to send to Jambo. On the other hand, the Kedi'ba Group would act in support of this operation. They were to lay an ambush at Ma'di'ba (Ogyiŋwa Junction) and also at Miṛi Loko, four miles north of Lui in support of the ambush at Ma'di'ba as well as at Lui, in case they failed to stop the movement of either the escapees to or the reinforcements from Mundri. The date and time of the attack was fixed at 6:00 am on Saturday, 19 June 1965 and civilians were warned to move away from the road on that day.

The Attack on Jambo/Mide Police Post

By 18 June, all units had taken their positions. Ezboni himself and other senior ranking leadership of the Anyanya at Mayaya moved near to Jambo to monitor the operation. They ordered that all civilians living along the Jambo-Lui-Mundri stretch of the road should move away on Saturday, 19 June. At Miṛi Loko, the Anyanya from Jackson's group at Kedi'ba took their positions. They broke the bridge on the small stream 200 meters down the road and positioned a locally made rocket launcher, *'Bu Diṛi,* with its turret aimed at the broken bridge. They also took position at Ma'di'ba to intercept any reinforcements that would attempt to rush from Mundri to aid the police at Jambo.

At Jambo (Mide), unfortunately, on 19 June at around 5:00 pm, four or five military trucks full of Government soldiers arrived Jambo from Yei. They were on their way to Maridi. The Anyanya unit poised to attack the police post early the next morning anxiously longed for their departure. But unfortunately, they decided to spend the night at Jambo. As is immediately clear, this drastically changed the military situation on the ground at Jambo. Now instead of two dozen or so members of the police unit with very light weapons, there now were more than 100 soldiers with much greater lethal power. Message was sent to Ezboni and the Anyanya senior commanders as to whether the attack should be called off, but the reply was negative. Part of the reason given for not calling off the attack was that the fighters positioned at Lui, Miṛi Loko and Ma'di'ba would be confused, since the Anyanya had no radio to communicate the change. Not calling off the attack in view of this change in the military situation on the ground was foolhardy to say the least. So, the operation was allowed to go ahead.

At Jambo (Mide), on the night of 18 June, the Anyanya crept near the police station and positioned their '*Bu Diṛi* gun, aiming it at the front of the police post. By 6:00 am, some of the policemen and soldiers had gathered in groups in front of the police post. They either were drinking tea or listening to the radio. At this moment, the Anyanya swung into action, firing the *Bu Diṛi* into the group of policemen and soldiers and the shell exploded in their midst. This was followed by small gun fire. Some of the policemen and soldiers were certainly injured or killed by the blast but no one could tell that for sure. But what followed was that, after recovering from the initial surprise, the soldiers quickly regrouped and launched a counter offensive in the direction from which the blast came. With their superior fire power and training, they quickly gained the upper hand and also in view of the fact that the Anyanya ran out of ammunition. The Anyanya had to run away, while losing one member.

On this same day, after the attack, the soldiers then split into two: while some remained with the police at Jambo, others took their injured to Mundri for treatment. As they were going, they possibly were surprised that there were no people along the whole length of the road from Jambo to Lui. And when they stopped at Lui, they probably also noticed that the few people they saw looked skittish and uneasy. They therefore must have concluded that the people were aware of what took place at Jambo some 28 miles away or that something sinister was afoot.

On the other hand, at Lui, those people who came near the army vehicles stated that the soldiers on the trucks stared at them in the most unfriendly way and they became frightened. Hence sensing something sinister, from Lui, the army began to move to Mundri very carefully and in a battle-ready formation. When they reached Miri Loko and using binoculars, they observed from a long distance that the small bridge next to Miri Loko had been broken. So, leaving the vehicles behind, they spread out on both sides of the road, out flanking the position the Anyanya had taken in wait for them. By the time the Anyanya became aware, they noted that the enemy was already behind them. They therefore fired the '*Bu Diri* in the direction of the bridge and fired a few rounds and ran away. The soldiers chased them and in the pursuit of the Anyanya, they shot dead one of the Anyanya soldiers, Ngola Dawidi from Kasiko. The same situation obtained to the other ambush at the Ma'di'ba Junction.

The soldiers were able to disperse the Anyanya unit deployed there and thereafter, they reached Mundri.

Army Retaliation and the Destruction of Lui

As mentioned above, when the army passed onwards to Mundri, they must have noted that the people looked skittish and in turn the people were frightened by the way the soldiers looked at them; and so, except for a few, many left the station that night. Even the patients in the hospital left their wards and went to sleep in the neighborhood. The very next day, Sunday 20 June 1965, the soldiers returned to Lui. At the same time, the small Anyanya contingent at Lui decided to go and take medicines for themselves from the hospital. They ordered the storekeeper to open the store, took sufficient medicines and loaded them on the hospital vehicle. One of them took the keys of the vehicle from the driver and drove it on the way to River Yei. But behind the small hill of Nyinyizo, the car broke down due to bad driving. They therefore called the driver of the vehicle to come and repair it.

While the Anyanya were busy with this, the soldiers were advancing on Lui; and from two miles outside the station, they disembarked from the trucks and moved on foot. Helped and guided by the policemen who formerly were at Lui and who knew the surroundings, they advanced in a pincer movement and surrounded the station. They took positions on the four main roads going out of the station. At around 10:00 am, beginning at the hospital, they began to shoot at the Anyanya soldiers still in the hospital. And thereafter they began to shoot indiscriminately, since they considered all the people who were still in the station were either Anyanya or their supporters. The few people who had remained in the station had to flee through the hills, the writer included. In the operation, the soldiers killed five civilians at Lui, one leprous woman, a shop boy and a family of three: father, mother and son. They burnt down many houses and ransacked the shops, the church offices and the hospital. From that day for the next seven years, Lui was abandoned and remained so until the Addis Ababa Agreement in 1972.

Lessons Learnt

Many lessons were learnt from this operation. Firstly, that the army was not a pushover as some Anyanya were wont to think at that time. Secondly, that the Anyanya soldier was in dire need of training. Thirdly, the Anyanya badly needed weapons, especially ammunition. Fourthly, the Anyanya needed intelligence and a fast (radio) means of communication. Fifthly, the operation showed that the two groups of the Anyanya, Mayaya and Kedi'ba Groups could work or synchronize their operations together despite their differences. This last one was what Ezboni wanted. On the part of the civilians, they came to realize that the army could kill anyone at sight, even if the person was unarmed, woman or child. In view of this, the people moved deep into the bush, away from the main roads, the writer included.

Positive Impact of Ezboni's Presence in the Anyanya

Now, Ezboni had spent about two months in the local Anyanya movement and his presence had a visible and significant impact on the situation in the area. Many things had definitely changed for the better, especially as regards the mistreatment of the people by the Anyanya. For example, the arrest, torture and even killing of suspected evil doers (*kole and mato*) ceased. The mistreatment and harassment of civilians declined substantially. Punishment of suspects without due process, be they suspected informers or persons accused of other crimes, also reduced markedly. Furthermore, some semblance of civilian administration had come into effect. Head Scouts and elders were required to judge both civil and criminal cases amongst the people instead of the Anyanya officers; drinking and merriment in the camps ceased; and food for the Anyanya was to be brought to the home of the Head Scout, rather than the soldiers going to civilian homes to demand food. And, although the operation at Jambo was not very successful, it had succeeded not only to make the Anyanya groups to cooperate together to face the common enemy but also gave them the first taste of frontal attack on the enemies. That incident, particularly the information that Ezboni was in the surrounding area, made the government to evacuate its last outlying the police post at Jambo and also compelled the government garrison in Mundri to adopt a defensive position, not venturing outside; in other words surrendering the whole of the Moru country side to the Anyanya.

Visit to Congo
Touching Base with Other Leaders

After the Jambo operation, his closest confidant Morris Ägyili strongly advised Ezboni not to expose himself in the front line as he had done at Jambo and suggested to him that the best thing for him to do was to join the other politicians like Fr. Saturnino, Joseph Oduho, Elia Lupe, Marko Rume and others in the Congo and/or Uganda. He told him that an escort could be provided to take him to Congo. Ezboni readily accepted that suggestion, since the suggestion fitted well with his own plans of going out to touch base with fellow politicians in Congo but would also enable him to find weapons and ammunition for the local Anyanya.

Hence in July 1965, Ezboni departed for the Congo accompanied by two sections of the Anyanya. But before his departure and in the presence of the writer, he instructed the Anyanya leadership who were present to allow students from the university and secondary schools to go back to school, when those institutions open, irrespective of whether they were in the Anyanya or not. He pointed out to them that there were enough people to fight the war and underlined the fact that the war was going to be fought by a combination of guns and the mind. This instruction made it possible for university students like Daniel Apollo, William Apaya and the writer to return to the university. This ended the first episode of Ezboni's involvement with the Anyanya.

Ezboni's Observations of Deficiencies in the Movement

According to him, his two or three months or so experience with the Moru Anyanya, he had made him notice several weaknesses with the resistance movement (political) and the fighting force (military). Firstly, there was a serious disconnect between the political leadership in Uganda and Congo with the fighting men (Anyanya) on the ground. The Anyanya leadership had no political education and had little awareness of what the reasons for fighting was all about, except to chase Mundukuru away. There were no political commissars assigned to the various areas to educate the combatants and enlighten the ordinary citizens on the goals of the fighting and the struggle. With no political leadership local Anyanya commanders became law unto themselves. Secondly, there was identifiable leadership and general headquarters of the force Major General Taffeng Lodongi at the top, Brigadier Ali Gbatala as the Deputy and Joseph Lagu as Chief of Staff, but there was poor or no communication between them. Also, there was not much of a chain of command from them to the area commanders in the various parts of Southern Sudan. Consequently, there was no overall military strategy for waging the war. Thirdly, the forces had no arms for fighting the war. Whatever were being bought from the Congolese forces or rebels using little money collected from the people were totally inadequate for fighting an established army as the government army.

Fourthly, there was no general administration to deal with the affairs of the civilians and as a result, the local Anyanya commanders took it up and made the worst out of it, especially since they were, in most cases, very poorly educated. In Moru land, he saw how the Anyanya commanders had taken up the role of the traditional chiefs and even killed (Chief Timon Biro an ex-MP) or humiliated them. Fifthly, both the political and military leadership did not travel to visit the many parts of Southern Sudan, even when they controlled the countryside. All those triggered in Ezboni the urge to reform and restructure both the political and military aspects of the struggle, if anything was to be achieved. He also considered that those obstacles could not be resolved from faraway countries and so the leadership must be inside the country in proximity to those problems.

With those in his mind, Ezboni set out to Angudri, an Anyanya operation center just on the Sudan-Congo border. There Ezboni was well received and respected because of his standing as a staunch nationalist and for the struggle he had waged all along for the sake of Southerners. During his stay, in Angudri, he had lengthy discussions with the Anyanya leadership there, among them were Captains William Hassan, Peter Cirillo and others. He told them about his vision of developing a general headquarters for the Anyanya, unifying and building it into an effective fighting force. At the end of two months in Angudri, he returned to Moru land but instead of returning to his home, he went to reside in Mayaya, the Anyanya Group D headquarters.

Actions After Return from Congo

"Truly I say to you, no prophet is acceptable in his hometown"

- St Luke 4:24

Response to an Appeal from the Elders and Chiefs in Kädiro

Upon arrival in the camp, Ezboni received an appeal, from the chiefs and elders of Kädiro, requesting him to come and save them from mistreatment by the Kedi'ba Anyanya Group under Jackson Garaŋwa.

Again this was at a time when Jackson himself was away with Ali Gbatala in Congo/Maridi area. Ezboni, who detested mistreatment of civilians by any Anyanya, responded promptly and ordered Major Aggrey Ndarago Andago and Morris Ägyili, the commander of the western bank, to proceed post-haste to Kädiro area to resolve that problem. The delegation went to Kedi'ba and according to Morris, quote, *"we arrested the situation by peaceful means with the chiefs, elders and the soldiers, without any problem and we brought some of the soldiers from the Kedi'ba Camp to the main camp at Mayaya to be integrated"*. Morris in the interview and in his written note emphatically stated that, when they went, there was neither violence nor any shooting during the whole performance of their mission to the Kedi'ba Camp. Furthermore, he underlined that those who were brought to the Mayaya camp were not considered and treated as prisoners, as some people were wont to say. Some of those who were brought to Mayaya camp included Kenneth Small, the brother of Commander Repent Sunday. However, before they could be integrated into the Mayaya Group and because they were free to move, some of them returned to Kedi'ba area and reconstituted their camp. Those who remained in the Mayaya camp were integrated into the main Group D Group. At this juncture, it is important to remember that, while those events, like the attack on the police post at Mide (Jambo) and the mission to Kädiro, were undertaken, Captain Repent Sunday was away. He had been sent earlier to search for weapons but had not returned for a very long time.

Ezboni's Second Military Operation, Attempt to Capture Mundri Garrison

In October 1965, Ezboni planned another military operation and this time the objective was to capture Mundri town. Mundri probably had a company size army unit deployed in it. The guerillas laid a siege to the town and every day they were tightening the noose and creeping closer and closer for the final assault. But the besieged soldiers called for air support and an aircraft came from Juba and strafed all around the town and so the besieging Anyanya had to run away.

Meeting with Elders and Chiefs of Kedi'ba

After the failure to capture Mundri, Ezboni visited the Kedi'ba area and according to McCall, he met with the chiefs and elders, where he told them that integration of the two Moru Anyanya groups was necessary; and that it was a good thing for the Moru people as well as for the whole Anyanya movement. During the meeting, the chiefs informed him that they had collected the sum of Ls 20,000 and given it to Jackson for the purchase of weapons but that Jackson had given it to Paul Ali Gbatala and that only a few weapons were purchased. Ezboni told them that since the area fell under Group D, the money should have been given to El Hag of the Commander of Group D in Mayaya and not to Gbatala of Group A. He promised to look into that matter. Following that meeting, the chiefs contributed another Ls 90 and gave it to a soldier who, instead of giving it to El Hag as per Ezboni's word, he took it to Jackson in the Congo, and reportedly Jackson, bought a bren gun with it. On his way back from Congo, Jackson had returned via Gbatala's camp in Maridi and as mentioned above, he earlier had complained bitterly to Gbatala about Ezboni's interference in his area of responsibility.

Emergence of Problems and Challenges
Difficulties with Jackson Garaŋwa

It can be said that at this time, Ezboni was now fully accepted and integrated into the Moru Anyanya, but had not completely succeeded in integrating its two sides. As had been mentioned previously, the antipathy between the Mayaya Anyanya (Group D) under El Hag Beshir and the Kedi'ba Anyanya under Jackson Garaŋwa predated Ezboni's arrival into Moru land. But his relationship with Jackson Garaŋwa grew increasingly strained over the issue of integration.

Ezboni's strong view was that the two wings of Anyanya should unite under Group D, a view that coincided with that of the Mayaya Group and which put him diametrically opposite to that of Jackson Garaŋwa, who loathed coming under El Hag's Group D. According to him, his conviction about unity under Group D was based on the following reasons: Firstly, the Mayaya Group was the one commissioned and launched by General Joseph Lagu to come and operate in Western Equatoria in Mundri area under El Hag and not under Ali Gbatala's Group A. Secondly, it was larger and comprised of professional and more mature soldiers than the Kedi'ba Group. Thirdly, for effective operations in Mundri area, the Anyanya forces needed to be under one command and which would directly strengthen the Anyanya in Moru land. Fourthly, the merger would help to curtail the excesses of Kedi'ba Group's misbehavior and mistreatment of the civilians. Those were his reasons for a merger; and as may be recalled, earlier he had attempted to integrate the two groups indirectly through the joint operation on the Jambo police post.

On the other hand, Jackson's anger with Ezboni could be traced to several reasons. As already mentioned above, Jackson saw Ezboni's joining the Mayaya Group and also pursuing the merger of the two Anyanya groups as fulfilling the agenda of his rivals. Secondly, as the supreme authority in the Kädiro area, he saw Ezboni's going to the area as well as dispatching a Mayaya mission to Kedi'ba to reconcile civilians with the Kedi'ba Anyanya as interference in his area of responsibility, especially when that was done in his absence. Thirdly, he also saw Ezboni's involvement of his troops in the joint operation on Jambo police post in his absence and consent as gross interference with his troops. Fourthly, he saw Ezboni's actions like: sending Aggrey and Morris to Kedi'ba in response to the appeal from the elders and chiefs; making efforts to integrate his troops into the Mayaya Group; and meeting with Kedi'ba elders and chiefs and giving them directives to send further contributions from the area to El Hag, done in his absence, as undermining his authority and tantamount to placing him under the Mayaya Group. In this, he even tried to call his group Group F. All those made him very angry and he now transferred the focus of his anger from his erstwhile protagonists, the leaders of the Mayaya Group, to Ezboni. As mentioned elsewhere, he had earlier complained bitterly to Ali Gbatala about Ezboni's interference in his area. Given all those above, and with Jackson insisting on his independence, the stage was set for a confrontation between him and Ezboni.

Action Against the Kedi'ba Camp

Upon arrival at his camp in Kedi'ba and after being told that Ezboni had met with the Kedi'ba area chiefs and elders, he ordered their arrest. When Ezboni heard of this, he was angry and in reaction, on 31 December 1965, he sent Repent Sunday, who had returned from Yei area, at the head of a force to bring the Kedi'ba camp under control. In the fighting, an unknown number of soldiers were killed on both sides and some of the Kedi'ba Group soldiers escaped to Lakes, while more others were taken prisoners. Ezboni emphasized that that was the most regrettable and the saddest episode in his life and it was also the darkest blemish on the life of the Moru Anyanya. As earlier narrated, that incident has been misinterpreted and wrongly projected by Jackson and some of Ezboni's detractors to be an action by Ezboni against the Kädiro people as a whole or by the Miza people against the Kädiro. Even McCall's book seems to imply that it was so. That is totally wrong. As is clear, that was entirely an Anyanya (military) affair and not a Miza versus Kädiro conflict.

Difficulties with Repent Sunday Gideon

As had also been mentioned earlier, Repent Sunday was away when Ezboni joined the Anyanya. He also was not present when Ezboni planned the operation on the Jambo police post and may be the operation to capture Mundri town as well. The exact time of his return to Mayaya, later Ngiṛi, is not known but it would appear that he had developed some grudge against Ezboni. It also would appear that, during his extended stay away from the Mayaya Group, he had come into contact with persons who were politically opposed to Ezboni in earlier years. Fuli in his book (pp 345) was of the opinion that he might have been influenced by Elisapana Käbi Mulla and his cousin Ezboni Jo'di, erstwhile political opponents of Ezboni. Now Repent's difference with Ezboni could also have been due to Ezboni's now towering political image in the area and a johnny-come-lately dabbling in military affairs and operations. According to McCall, he also might have resented being ordered by Ezboni to go to Kedi'ba to free the chiefs who had been arrested by Jackson Garaŋwa, if necessary, by force. After freeing the chiefs and dispersing the Kedi'ba camp, he must have returned to the Mayaya camp with the conviction that Ezboni was a problem. Consequently, he immediately ordered the arrest of Ezboni Mondiri and Aggrey Andago and had their hands tied up. He also sent soldiers to arrest Morris Ägyili from the battle front near Mundri. According to Morris, he was brought to the camp and his hands were also tied up behind his back by Sergeant Stanley Kariŋwa; and this was followed by severe beatings. The charge against them, according to Morris, was a very strange one and as well as a very dubious one. It was that they were "fighting the Arab government soldiers". In Ezboni's words, this was the first humiliation he suffered at the hands of his own people. After two days as prisoners, Repent Sunday and his group decided to send them to Angudri to be tried. But on arrival, no charges could be found against the trio and so, they were released and told that they were free to return to Moru land.

CHAPTER VIII:
IN THE GOVERNMENT OF AZANIA LIBERATION FRONT (ALF)

The ALF before Ezboni joined
Oduho deposes Aggrey Jaden and forms ALF

While Ezboni was busy trying to improve, and unify the Moru Anyanya, significant developments were happening in the political leadership of the Southern Resistance Movement outside. As already narrated in Chapter V, Oduho had already taken the leadership of the Movement and declared himself the President of his new party the Azania Liberation Front' (ALF). He named the Cabinet and appointed Taffeng Major General and the overall Commander of the Anyanya forces, with Brigadier Ali Gbatala as his Deputy and Joseph Lagu as the Secretary for Special Functions. In the new arrangement, Fr. Saturnino remained as the Patron of the Movement. Also, as regards to the new party, Oduho went on to declare that, henceforth, the headquarters of the Movement must be located and has also to operate from within Southern Sudan. He therefore established his headquarters at Dito, on top of Lomohidang Hill above Isoke; Patron Fr. Saturnino based himself at Tul; while the military, under Taffeng was based at Lorifa. All those locations were in the Latuka Mountains, except for the Secretariat, headed by Severino Fuli, which was based at the Loreze camp in Ma'di area. Therefore, as can be seen, the headquarters of the ALF Government was very scattered. As the President, Oduho took a tour of Eastern Equatoria from January to March 1966. After his return, he convened a meeting of the leadership of ALF to be held at Tul, where the Patron was residing.

On the Way to the ALF Meeting
Selection of Lomileŋwa as GHQ for the Anyanya

Ezboni heard about this meeting and very much longed to be part of it. Additionally, he longed to meet the new leadership of the Movement (ALF). He particularly was excited about Joseph Oduho's declaration that the Movement should operate from within Southern Sudan, since that coincided with his views. So, he hurried there via Angudri in the Congo. While in Angudri, Ezboni put forward his views to the Anyanya leadership there saying that, for the Anyanya to succeed, it must have a centralized command which should be located in one place; and that such a location should by necessity be inside the Sudan. He also told them that Angudri was not suitable for such headquarters because it was almost in the Congo. He therefore selected a place called Lomileŋwa in Moru land, a spot lying between Chief Jambo and Chief Ngere's areas (Sketch

Sketch II: Approximate Location of Lomileŋwa Anyanya General Headquarters (Not to Scale)

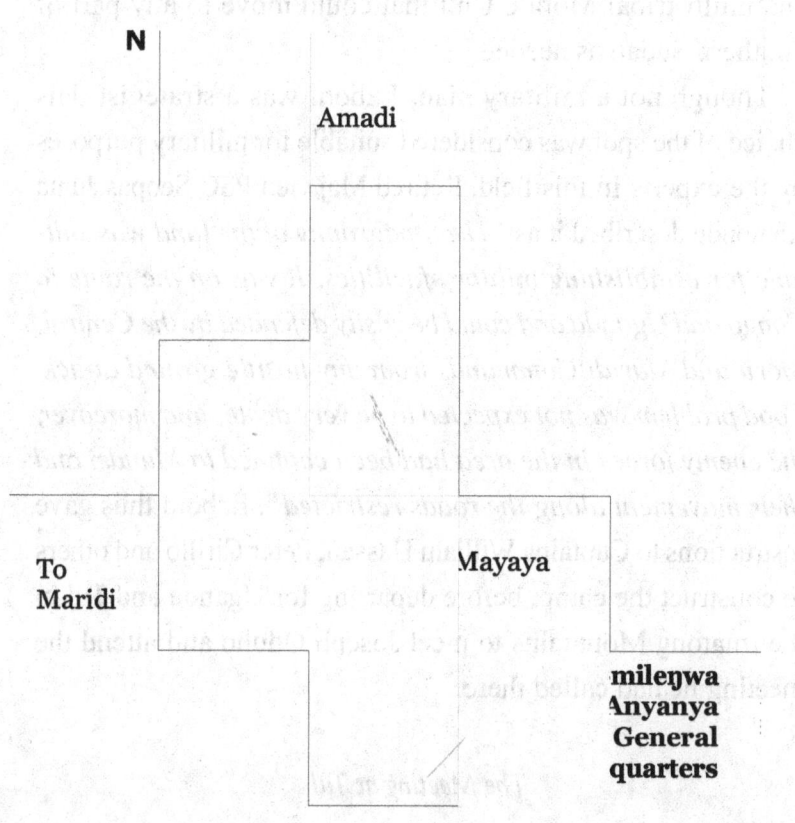

II). The location was also very near the Pojulu and Nyangwara areas of the Central Command and near a permanent source of water. He envisaged Lomileŋwa to have soldiers from all tribes and all parts of Southern Sudan, in addition to being a General Headquarters for the Anyanya. Lomileŋwa would also house the training of the forces as well as a base for a well-equipped and multi-tribal Mobile Unit that could move to any part of Southern Sudan as needed.

Though not a military man, Ezboni was a strategist. His choice of the spot was considered suitable for military purposes by the experts in this field. Retired Maj Gen PSC Scopas Juma Kamonde described it as *"The topography of the land was suitable for establishing military facilities. It was on the route to Congo and Uganda and could be easily defended by the Central, Moru and Maridi Commands from any hostile ground attack. Food problem was not expected to be very acute; and moreover, the enemy forces in the area had been confined to Mundri and their movement along the roads restricted"*. Ezboni thus gave instructions to Captains William Hassan, Peter Cirillo and others to construct the camp, before departing for Uganda and Tul in the Imatong Mountains to meet Joseph Oduho and attend the meeting he had called there.

The Meeting at Tul

The meeting duly took place in the period 08-22 March 1966. Ezboni's unexpected arrival and contribution greatly enhanced the outcome of that meeting. The information about his substantial contribution to that meeting, in terms of ideas, has come from two sources: the first source is from firsthand information by

Severino Fuli in his book "*Shaping a Free Southern Sudan*" and the second one from Storrs McCall's manuscripts "*The making of the Anyanya insurgency in Southern Sudan*" and now published into a book "*The Genesis and Struggle of the Anyanya in Southern Sudan*" by Storrs McCall and Lam Akol. The two versions (Fuli's and McCall's) are, however, very close in their description of what took place in that meeting. In his book, Severino Fuli had these to say, quote:

"*Mr. Ezboni Mondiri after hearing that both the political Movement and the Military wing would operate within the Sudan, traveled from Zaire to Uganda and to Tul where he met the President, the Patron, Joseph Lagu, the Secretary for Special Functions and others. Mr. Mondiri on the spot was appointed Secretary for Defence for the Azania Movement. They met and discussed and came up with a skeleton of "working programme" of the Movement as detailed below:*

i. *Make the Anyanya converge into Azania Nation under one strong army which would have its main objective that of fighting the liberation war, streamlining the ranks throughout the Azania nation which comprise all the three Provinces of Equatoria, Bahr El Ghazal and Upper Nile*

ii. *Establish civil administration in Azania liberated areas for effective administration free from Anyanya interference, all the way down from Governor to Scouts (posts created by the Anyanya). Each Province in the South was reconstituted into smaller Provinces. The former was broken into Torit and Kapoeta, forming East Equatoria Province; Juba and Yei forming Central Equatoria Province; Maridi and Yambio, Western Equatoria Province*" (Note: no mention of the breakdown of the Provinces of Bahr El Ghazal and

> *Upper Nile). All proceeds derived from civil administration were to be used for waging war*
>
> iii. *The Secretary for Defence was to travel and implement the programme throughout South Sudan, commencing in Equatoria and then going to the other two Provinces".*

While Severino gave descriptive narration of what took place in that meeting, McCall provided a more analytical contribution of Ezboni to ALF. That is, the meeting of 08 to 22 March 1966 was quote *"marked by the emergence of Secretary for Defence, Ezboni Mondiri, as the most dynamic member of the Government. Mondiri was responsible for the most original idea(s) to come out of the ALF. This was the replacement of the old colonial division of the South into three provinces and 21 districts by a new division into eight regions, a region being smaller than a province but larger than a district. The purpose of this division was to facilitate administration in a country which was immense enough in the days of the British, but which has been made much more immense by the breakdown of all forms of communication, except travel on foot. In such condition the effective administration of an area the size of a province was impossible. Mondiri's idea of dividing the country into regions proved a popular one, and has been adopted in one form or another by various provisional governments (of the Movement) that have existed since".* It was also adopted by President Nimeiri after the Addis Ababa Agreement.

Ezboni joins the ALF Government as the Secretary for Defence
Tasks and Challenges of the Assignment

After the meeting at Tul, Ezboni, as the Secretary for Defence, had now tasks in both military and civil administrative fields. He now also found himself among the top leadership of the Movement and with huge responsibilities. Nonetheless, he said he was happy because at last, the assignment was going to give him the opportunity to put into practice what he had long cherished to do, that is, to meld Southern Sudan to be an independent African nation. He therefore plunged into the work with gusto. As had also been mentioned elsewhere,

But Ezboni's ascendancy to that position of power in the Movement sent a chill up the spines of the Northern political establishment in Khartoum. Several papers blamed Sir El Khatim's transitional government for allowing Ezboni to go to the South, after resigning the Cabinet post. To them, with Ezboni in the Anyanya, the government should expect the Anyanya to be a more formidable foe.

Ezboni's Vision and Mission

Based on what he saw in Moru land, one of Ezboni's priorities was to separate the military from the civilian affairs; and in order to achieve that, it was necessary to entrust civil administration in the hands of qualified and experienced administrators, instead of the poorly educated Head Scouts. For this to be effective, he visualized that the size of the administrative units, provinces or regions, should be smaller so as to be manageable. He conceived the number to be to seven:[9] three in Equatoria and two each in Upper Nile and Bahr El Ghazal. In his view those regions or provinces should be run by a Governor, assisted by District Commissioners in each of the 21 districts of the three southern provinces.

On the military side, Ezboni's view and objective was that the Anyanya should be built into a national army, just as national armies are globally. It should have a national outlook, rather than the existing tribally based fighting forces with parochial outlooks that did not go beyond the local and/or tribal boundaries. For that reason, he envisaged that there should be one General Army Headquarters for the Anyanya at Lomileŋwa, which then was under construction at his request; and that in each of the new regions/provinces, there should be a Military Commander with a headquarter unit and companies, the number of which would be determined by size and activity in that region. Those views dictated the resolutions called the **New Policy Program for ALF** and Ezboni must have been delighted to be tasked to disseminate and operationalize them throughout Southern Sudan.

Tour to Disseminate and Operationalize the ALF New Policy Program
The first leg, Eastern Equatoria

According to Fuli, the dissemination of the New Policy Program began as soon as the meeting closed. Now armed with the above

---

9   It is not known why he proposed Equatoria to be divided into three and Upper Nile and Bahr El Ghazal to only be divided into two

New Policy Program, President Oduho and Ezboni traveled together to explain it to the re-confirmed overall Anyanya Commander, Maj Gen Taffeng Lodongi at Lorifa. Taffeng welcomed and approved it. From Lorifa, President Oduho and Ezboni travelled to Dito, the home base of Oduho, where the B Company under Lazarus Mutek was based. Lazarus also accepted the New Policy Program. Oduho remained at Dito but Ezboni and Joseph Lagu proceeded to Loreze in Ma'di land; and Lagu explained the New Policy Program to Group D[10] and the people accepted it. Ezboni was now to cross the Nile to explain the same to the Anyanya and people in Central and Western Equatoria and beyond. It was however felt that, at least one person from Eastern Equatoria should accompany him in order to give credence to his message. Lagu chose Severino Fuli to accompany Ezboni because of his stature but Fuli declined. His reason was that he did not want to work with or under Oduho (ALF), because of some previous misunderstanding. But Ezboni pleaded with him, reminding him of the days of the Federal Party in Khartoum and Fuli accepted to accompany Ezboni in his tour.

At this juncture, it is to be underscored that we are very grateful to Fuli for meticulously keeping a record of Eboni's encounters in the six- month tour on foot of the area up to Central and Western Equatoria. So, from Fuli's account, the tour went as follows:

---

10   Not to be confused with the Group D in Moru land

Plate V: Severino Fuli, Ezboni's travelling companion and Executive of the SANU, ALF and SSLM Secretariat. Much is owed to him for meticulous records of the Movements and especially the travel with Ezboni (Courtesy Taban Avelino)

Urugi Village, East Bank

Having already explained the New Policy Program to units in Latuka land, Ezboni explained the same to a gathering of the Ma'di people. The people were very appreciative and upon hearing it, an old man blessed Ezboni and stated that his mission tour would succeed. Ezboni then crossed the Nile to the west bank.

Second Leg, Central Equatoria
Shukole

Ezboni then crossed the Nile to the western bank to Shukole. The people there were a mixture of Ma'di and Kuku. After hearing of the new administration and the New Policy Program, the people expressed their happiness and appreciation of the New Policy. They honored Ezboni's presence by slaughtering a bull for a feast.

Pengkimang Camp

This Anyanya camp was located on the west bank of the Nile among the Kuku. It was commanded by a Saturnino and was deputized by Bismarck 'Bungit. Before the briefng, Ezboni asked for the veteran politician, Marko Rume, who lived in the area. After the arrival of Marko, Ezboni explained the new ALF administration and the New Policy Program. The attendants greatly appreciated the New Policy, especially the separation of the military from civilian affairs. At Ezboni's request, Marko Rume, a master spinner who could easily win hearts and minds of the people, agreed to join the team for the onward journey.

Nyambiri (10-12 July 1966)

Ezboni addressed a very large crowd comprising of the Anyanya, the chiefs and ordinary civilians. In the ensuing discussions, the concerns voiced included: the involvement of the soldiers (Anyanya) in civilian administration and affairs; the failure of the political leadership to avail the wherewithal for prosecuting the war; and the rivalry among the political leadership that was weakening the Movement. In response, Ezboni told the attendants that the New Policy Program was aimed at addressing those concerns. Subsequently, with inputs from Fuli and Marko, the attendants endorsed the New Policy Program and requested Marko to represent their views in the meeting which Ezboni will be holding at their Central Command Headquarters of Central Equatoria.

Nyambiri Group 2 Headquarters

At Nyambiri, since both the commander and his deputy were away, Ezboni's team was received by the third officer in command. He received the delegation with some high degree of threats and suspicion. Nonetheless, after a while, his attitude changed and Ezboni explained to them the new ALF administration and his position in it as the Secretary for Defence. He also explained to them the New Policy Program, which they appreciated and supported.

Abugo (28 July 1966)

Abugo was the base of Group C, located among the Kakwa on the Gbula, Sudan/Congo border. The Group C Commanding Officer was David Dada. In his briefing to David, Ezboni told him about the changes that had taken place in the leadership of the Movement and about the New Policy Program. He further told him that the New Policy Program had been approved by the people and groups on the east bank as well as by the two

Companies at Pengkimang and Nyambiri. Thereafter, they both agreed to hold a bigger meeting of all the commanders of the Central Command at Abugo to be held on 10 August 1966.

On 10 August, the meeting was duly held and it attended by several Commanding officers of Central Equatoria, namely, David Dada, Clement Wani, Simon Jada and Philip Angotowa and the prominent political leaders of Central Equatoria were also present. Ezboni explained the change in leadership from Aggrey Jaden to Joseph Oduho and the ALF set up. He elaborated on the New Policy Program under the new leadership. In the ensuing discussions, the attendants criticized the manner in which Oduho seized power from Aggrey, but accepted that the New Policy Program was a good thing. After additional words from Marko Rume and Severino Fuli, the meeting accepted the change in leadership as well as the New Policy Program, and accordingly passed the following resolutions: The New Policy Program was accepted in its entirety.

i. *Political leaders should bury their differences and it was strongly recommended that the Movement provide war logistics for the Anyanya.*
ii. *New Central Command Headquarters was to be set up which would embody and incorporate both Mobile Force and Training wings.*
iii. *With regards to civil administration, the meeting nominated Mr. Daniel Jumi Tongun Governor of Central Province and the Secretary of Defence appointed him in absentia, while on official function in Aba, Zaire. He was told to set up a working machinery for Civil Administration without delay.*

iv. The above resolutions were put in writing addressed to Anyanya High Command and the Commander of Central Command and Civil Administration Authorities.

According to Fuli and from Ezboni himself, the attendants were very satised with the meeting and they departed.

Group B Company Outpost 14 August

The outpost was near Mitika. The Company was under Major Adam. Ezboni informed them of the changes in leadership of the Movement and the programs of the New Policy which was well received and supported. The delegation then entered Zaire (Congo) to Kagiko.

Third Leg, Meetings in Congo, Including with Leaders of Bahr El Ghazal and Upper Nile

Ezboni's purpose of entering into the Congo was twofold: to meet Daniel Jumi who was residing in Aba; and to brief the Bahr El Ghazal (Dinka) and Upper Nile political and military leadership who at that time were residing in Congo. In meeting them in Congo, that would save him the journey of travelling to Bahr El Ghazal and Upper Nile. It is to be mentioned that, many of those leaders were in Congo to purchase weapons. But in the case of Bahr El Ghazal, the Dinka politico-military leadership were actually residing in the camps in the Congo.

Kagiko, Congo

This was an outpost of the Anyanya inside the Congo and was used for the purchase and bartering of weapons. Eliaba Surur was residing there. Ezboni briefed him about the ALF government and its New Policy Program, which he received well.

Aba Town, Congo 18 August

In Aba, Ezboni met Daniel Jumi and briefed him fully about the changes that brought ALF at the leadership of the Movement with Oduho as the President; with himself as the Secretary for Defence; and the task given him. He informed him about the New Policy Program and the overwhelming support the change and the New Policy had received in both Eastern and Central Equatoria. He told him of his plan to continue the mission in Western Equatoria and the other provinces. Daniel expressed his full support for the change and the New Policy Program. Ezboni then told him that in the big meeting at Abugo, the leaders of Central Equatoria had nominated him, Daniel Jumi, to be their Governor in the new administrative set up; and he, in accordance to the powers given him, there and then appointed Daniel Jumi as the Governor for Central Equatoria. He instructed Daniel to get in touch with David Dada, the overall Commander in Central Equatoria so that they could begin work in the new province.

Since Ezboni wanted to meet with the Dinka politico-military leaders in Congo, he asked Daniel Jumi, who was well- known to the local Congo government authorities, to assist him to be allowed to hold meetings with the Dinka leaders in the camps. He also asked Daniel Jumi to introduce him to the Dinka leaders, with whom he, Daniel, was well acquainted. Daniel obliged and made the contacts and so a meeting was called with the Bahr El Ghazal leaders.

Meeting with Bahr El Ghazal and Upper Nile Leadership at Aba, Congo

Ezboni then held a meeting with the politico-military leadership from Bahr El Ghazal and Upper Nile and who were resident in Congo. The meeting was also attended by very many people from other parts of the Southern Sudan. In that meeting, Ezboni's delegation comprised of Marko Rume, Severino Fuli and Daniel Jumi. Ezboni told the gathering of the following: the changes that had brought Oduho as the President of the Movement; of his being appointed as Secretary for Defence; and of Joseph Lagu being appointed as Chief of Staff for the Anyanya. He went on to explain the program of the New Policy and the purpose of his mission tour. He told them that, at a later date, he would be going to Upper Nile and Bahr El Ghazal to execute the task given him; but that in the meantime, he was requesting those leaders present to pass on this information to their respective home areas. Subsequently, the other three members of the delegation underscored the importance of unity among Southerners in order to get rid of Arab domination.

In the ensuing discussions, the attendants welcomed and supported the new leadership as well as the New Policy Program and agreed to send armed scouts ahead of the mission to sensitize the people in their respective places. Thereafter, on 05 August, the delegation headed back to Southern Sudan.

Angudri

Angudri, was an Anyanya transit camp in Avokaya land, just inside the Sudan border. It was under the command of El Hag Beshir, formerly of Group D, (the Mayaya Group). On 27 August, Ezboni addressed the troops in Angudri, explaining the change in leadership and the New Policy Program. Thereafter, he, Fuli and El Hag left for Brig. Paul[11] Ali Gbatala's camp in Maridi area. On the way, Ezboni continued to brief the people along the way about the New Policy Program, wherever they stopped to rest or sleep.

Fourth Leg, Western Equatoria
Ibba, 16 September 1966

After some days, Ezboni and delegation arrived Brig. Paul Ali Gbatala's base in Ibba. He was happy to receive Ezboni's delegation.

Prior to a general meeting, Ezboni gave a detailed briefing to Paul Ali on both the military and political changes that had taken place and of the overwhelming support for those changes in Eastern and Central Equatoria. He also told him of the support of the Upper Nile and Bahr El Ghazal groups in the Congo for the New Program. He then told Paul Ali of his wish to hold a big meeting in the Ibba area and proposed that, in the interest of time, if Paul could send a message Yambio for the Zande Anyanya to send representatives to attend that meeting. Paul Ali

---

11   Ali Gbatala, a Muslim, but now converted to Christianity. He took the name Paul.

Plate VI: Brigadier Paul Ali Gbatala, NCO in the Sudan Defence Force in Torit. He did not surrender and continued to fight the government in the forests of Maridi and Congo; and was the Deputy to Lt. General Taffeng Lodongi until Gen Joseph Lagu took over in 1971

appreciated the developments that had taken place but refused Ezboni's request to send a message to Yambio/Zande Anyanya[12]

---

12   As will be explained later, the Azande, having been disappointed with the political (SANU) leadership in the east, had set up their own political leadership and an Anyanya Command with no connection to the east. They considered their area to comprise of Tambura, Yambio and Maridi. For that reason, some of the Maridi political leadership like Michael Ngamunde were part of that Azande political-military set up. Ali Gbatala occupied a position in the middle. While accepting the SANU leadership in the east, he also accepted to cooperate with the Azande/Yambio Group. So he declined Ezboni's request to send a message to the Azande/Yambio group, lest it

to send representatives to the meeting. He, however, agreed to send messages to his internal sub-groups to send five officers each to attend the meeting.

The Ibba Meeting, 21-22 September 1966

As compared to the others the meeting in Ibba according to Fuli, was a rather difficult one. Ezboni told the attendants of the change of leadership that had taken place from Aggrey Jaden (SANU) to Joseph Oduho (ALF) and of his position in that government as the Secretary for Defence. He told them of the New Policy Program and the task given to him to operationalize it and which had brought him to Ibba area. At the end of his speech, he concluded by announcing to the attendants that the overall Anyanya General Headquarters will be based in Western Equatoria and that will be in addition to the Western Command Headquarters. He did not disclose the locations of those headquarters.

In the ensuing discussion a query was raised by political officer/administrator, Simon Mondisi as to what crime did Aggrey Jaden do to deserve removal from the leadership? He also wanted Oduho to account for the Movement's funds of 1961-1964. In his interjection, Brig Paul Ali Gbatala complained that, unlike the military, the politicians have always let down the people of Southern Sudan. He warned the politicians and stated that they the politicians should let them, the military, do their duties of liberating the South from Arab domination. He concluded his speech by reiterating a further warning to

---

jeopardizes his relationship with them.

the political leaders about communism. (NB: this warning by Ali Gbatala particularly about communism is very significant. It revealed how far wide the misinformation by the missionaries had spread; and alleging that the Southern students in the University of Khartoum had all become communists. This misinformation also been mentioned by Hilary Logali in his memoirs.[13] As will be seen later, this same misinformation was used to incarcerate as well as to deny Ezboni participation in the Second National Convention in Angudri in February 1967). Ezboni responded to the query of Simon and the statement by Paul Ali Gbatala.

In view of the apparent skepticism in the expressions of Paul Ali and Simon, Severino Fuli expounded on what Ezboni had conveyed and told them that both Eastern and Central Equatoria had embraced the change and the New Policy Program and that, as a member from far off Eastern Equatoria, he would want to take back a positive response from them. After this appeal, the attendants accepted and endorsed the messages from Ezboni and drew up the following resolutions:

a. *That while the Ibba meeting of Western Equatoria wholeheartedly welcomed the New Policy Program of the Azania Movement, the meeting deplored and warned against illegal seizure of powers which the people would not condone in future. The Anyanya leadership set up under Major General Emidio Taffeng Lodongi and Brigadier Paul Gbatala had been confirmed and any change in plan in leadership will be resisted*
b. *That all political leaders who are in the liberation movement should and ways and means to supply logistics for the war effort*

---

13   Soon to be published.

c. The meeting agreed and recommended that the Western Command Headquarters, including both a mobile and training wings, be established forthwith. Henceforth, the Anyanya should concentrate in the liberation war without interference from sister partner, the civil administrative services.
d. Approved separate establishment of civil service in all liberated areas (Western Province inclusive) under provincial Governors with full administrative staff with functional structural system to raise funds for utilization and in meeting the Anyanya needs
e. The Ibba meeting had learned from the Defence Secretary about the establishment of the Anyanya General Headquarters in the Western Province, apart from the Western Command Headquarters. The meeting failed to understand the logic for this unprecedented setup and demanded clarification from Azania headquarters
f. The Defence Secretary should adequately communicate to the Yambio Command in writing about the changes and send extracts from other previous meetings that had led up to it.

Those resolutions were endorsed with jubilation. Paul Ali Gbatala, now conrmed as the overall Deputy Chief Commander to Taffeng Lodongi by the Secretary for Defence, made a big farewell meal for the delegation. He thanked Ezboni and requested Fuli, who was due to return to Eastern Equatoria, to take the following message to his overall head Anyanya Commander, Taffeng Lodongi *"Please, tell him that now is the time to show our capabilities and determination to the Arabs. Let them know for sure that we mean business and want to see the South free"*.

Fuli promised to deliver the message when he got back. Ezboni thanked Paul Ali Gbatala for the hospitality and the meal ended with prayers. On 24 September 1966, Ezboni's delegation departed the Ibba area.

It is noteworthy to observe here that, of all the meetings Ezboni had with the Anyanya and people of Eastern and Central Equatoria, the Ibba and Nyambiri meetings were the ones where the attendants had expressed reservations and/or concerns regarding the new dispensation. From reading McCall's and Alison Magaya's books, the skepticism and behavior of Paul Ali Gbatala and company had most likely emanated from the ambivalent position they were in. That was, in addition being a deputy to Taffeng, he and the Maridi Anyanya were allied and were part of the Azande Anyanya. In fact, most of their senior politicians were members of the Azande Anyanya political leadership. As is known, the Azande Anyanya had maintained a separate and independent Command from the other Anyanya groups to the east of them. They only joined the rest fully in 1969, when Joseph Lagu included Samuel Abu John in the Anyanya Military High Command.

Final Leg

Homeward Bound, Arrival and Settling to Work

From Ibba, Ezboni walked northeastwards to Moru land and according to Fuli, wherever Ezboni passed, the people gave him a tumultuous welcome. But to the disappointment of Fuli, he addressed the people in Moru language, which meant that, Fuli could not get exactly what he was saying. However, it was most likely that he was repeating what he had been telling the other communities elsewhere. Thence, after four weeks, they reached the new Anyanya National General Headquarters (GHQ) at Lomileŋwa.

Appointment of Elisapana Mulla as Governor for Western Equatoria Province

As mentioned earlier, one of Ezboni's tasks was the appointment of the Governors in the new provinces. Using that authority, he already had appointed Daniel Jumi as the Governor of Central Equatoria. For the newly created Western Equatoria Province, his intention was to appoint Elisapana Käbi Mulla as the Governor for Western Equatoria. Elisapana was a Local Government Executive Officer and who at that time had escaped from the government service and was residing in his home in Chief Jambo's area. Upon arrival at Lomileŋwa, Ezboni learnt that Elisapana was about to go back to government service, just as Gordon Sworo, another experienced Local Government Executive Officer had done.

Ezboni promptly sent an urgent letter to Elisapana requesting him to come and meet him immediately. Elisapana duly arrived and Ezboni narrated to him the new developments in the Movement and those were: the change from SANU to ALF under Joseph Oduho; the New Policy Program; his (Ezboni's) appointment as Secretary for Defence for the Movement; the mandate given him to reorganize the Anyanya force; and to set up the administration by appointing Governors in the newly created Provinces. He told him that, using that mandate, he already had appointed Daniel Jumi as Governor for Central Equatoria. He then asked Elisapana's consent to be appointed as the first Governor for Western Equatoria. In response, Elisapana asked to be given 24 hours to make up his mind, which he did and accepted the position. Ezboni thus appointed Elisapana Käbi Mulla as the first Anyanya Governor for Western Equatoria Province.

Visit to Chief Ngere's Area

As Fuli was now ready to go back to Ma'di land in Eastern Equatoria, Ezboni accompanied him across River Yei to the home of an Anyanya Head Scout by the name of Komoyangi. There, he addressed a group of people but spoke in Moru, so again Fuli could not follow what he said. However, Fuli was astonished to see Ezboni suddenly stand up and 'rain blows' to the head of the Head Scout. Fuli did not understand why and was very much shocked. We can only surmise that Komoyangi might have uttered or questioned something which Ezboni did not like. This incident gives a glimpse into the character of Ezboni. He did not suffer fools easily; and when angry over failure to perform or deliver, he could impulsively strike at the source of the anger. As could be recalled, this impulsive characteristic was probably the reason that made him slap or shake up the Northern telephone operator in early 1965. And as it may be recalled, that incident led to his resignation from the Ministry of Transport and Communication in Khartoum. In view of what he saw, Fuli reproached him for such behavior. Nonetheless, since Fuli was departing, he thanked him for his companionship and on 05 November 1966, Fuli departed for his home after traveling for four months with Ezboni through the wilderness of Southern Sudan. Ezboni then returned to Lomileŋwa to settle down to tackle the huge assignment in front of him.

Settling Down to Work at Lomileŋwa GHQ

As may be recalled from an earlier paragraph, Ezboni had selected Lomileŋwa as the GHQ for the Anyanya. After its construction, it was placed under Captain William Hassan. Other officers there with William included Peter Cirillo, Aggrey Andago, Emmanuel Abur, Morris Ägyili among others. Soon the GHQ began to take shape as well as to receive soldiers from many parts of the three Southern Provinces. So, after the long tour, Ezboni settled down to work at Lomileŋwa. His primary objective was to meld the disparate Anyanya groups into one disciplined army. He, therefore, planned to hold a big convention for all Anyanya commanders at Lomileŋwa and began to make contacts for it. In Upper Nile, he wrote a letter to Senior Commanders Paul Awet, Paul Adut and Paul Nyigori, inviting them to the convention. Paul Nyigori acknowledged the invitation but the other two did not respond. In Bahr El Ghazal, he paid a visit to the Anyanya camps in Lakes (Rumbek area) in January 1967, where he was well received. There, he informed them about the convention and appointed Commander Philip Nanga as the overall Commander for the whole of Bahr El Ghazal. He also recruited a very large number of Dinka soldiers for the General Headquarters at Lomileŋwa.

Ezboni's other concern as Secretary for Defence was how to get arms for the Anyanya. He was acutely aware that, the few light weapons which the Anyanya were purchasing from the Congo rebels would never be sufficient to defeat the government army deployed all over Southern Sudan. He also was aware that the Government of the Sudan had undertaken a wide and successful diplomatic offensive with the surrounding African countries to the extent that none of them would extend arms to the Anyanya, leave alone allowing arms to transit through their countries to Southern Sudan. In view of those, he toyed with the idea of getting arms from China, which at that time was supplying arms to other freedom fighters elsewhere in Africa, for example, insurgents like of South Africa, Angola and Mozambique. In pursuit of that, he drafted a letter to the leader of China, requesting weapons for the Anyanya. It is quite certain that, given the remoteness of Lomileŋwa, that letter did not leave Lomileŋwa or even reach the Chinese. But that draft letter, as we shall see later, was used against him as a proof of his being a communist.

CHAPTER IX:
COUP AND THE END OF ALF GOVERNMENT

Conspiracy and Coup against Ezboni and ALF
The Coup Plot

Upon return to Lomileŋwa from Lakes, Ezboni was confronted by rebellion and *coup de etat* on 20 February 1967. The person who was to overthrow him was an ex-seminarian Ferdinand Goi,[14] a Balanda Bviri from Bessalia near Wau and his story is the following. Ferdinand left Wau and came to Congo and thence to Angudri, where Paul Ali Gbatala was. According

---

14   He was in the seminary in Milan, Italy, where in 1962 he made contacts with SANU in Congo. He returned to Wau; informed the people of his plans; and joined the Anyanya in May 1963. A radical, he overthrew Filberto Ucini then the leader of the Anyanya in Western Bahr El Ghazal. After some activities in the Tambura area, he went to Congo and was involved in the coup.

to Retired General Scopas Juma, while in Congo, Ferdinand *"received some help, assumed to have been given by some Verona Fathers"* for the coup against ALF and Ezboni. And either knowingly or unknowingly, Paul Ali Gbatala, who as mentioned earlier was the second in command to Taffeng Lodongi, had transferred Repent Sunday from Group D (Ngiṛi of the Moru Anyanya Headquarters), first to Maridi and then to Angudri. At Angudri, Repent Sunday found common cause with Goi and Camillo Odongi and plotted the coup against ALF and Ezboni. They even succeeded to convince Paul Ali Gbatala to sign the document, declaring the overthrow of Ezboni and ALF. In the plot, Repent Sunday was to use his forces at Ngiṛi to attack the GHQ at Lomileŋwa and they would be augmented by a force from Angudri, led by Ferdinand. But the plot was discovered. On hearing of the plot against him and ALF, Ezboni hurried to Angudri; and Repent Sunday, upon hearing of Ezboni's coming, slipped back to Moru land to the forces at Ngiṛi which began to attack Lomileŋwa.

Anatomy of the Coup

McCall relates that what followed was however very difficult to unravel but we shall attempt to reconstruct what actually took place from three sources: from McCall, who claimed to have obtained it from Francis Wajo, Ezboni Jodi, Elisapana Käbi Mulla and Gordon Mourtat; from Retired Major General Scopas Juma Kamonde, who was an eye witness to the events because he was in the company of Ezboni on his way from Angudri to Lomileŋwa GHQ; and from Morris Ägyili, also an eye witness and who was with Ezboni throughout those events. While McCall's version could be obtained in his book, both General Scopas Kamonde and Morris Ägyli's versions are from their own hand-written notes of what they witnessed. Therefore, in order to piece together the full story, we will first present McCall's version as an overall summary of the events and fill it up with versions from Major General Scopas Juma and Morris Ägyili. We will deal with the underlying reasons in the ensuing paragraphs.

McCall's Version

According to McCall: *"Some say the coup was instigated by the Roman Catholics who disliked Mondiri for his alleged communist connections; and so with the death of Fr. Saturnino, a month earlier, they had lost their principal person in the Movement. Others say that it represented merely a desire on the part of certain Anyanya officers to get rid of civilian politicians above them. In any case, the principal military participant appears to have been Ferdinand Goi, (the ex- seminarian), Camillo Odongi and Repent Sunday, who had persuaded Paul Ali Gbatala, the senior officer at Angudri, to sign a declaration stating that the army had taken over the government from ALF. No sooner had the document been signed, however, confusion set in. Goi was chosen to take the declaration to Mondiri in Lomileŋwa, accompanied by some Dinka soldiers. But on the way, the group met two Dinka friends of Mondiri who persuaded the other Dinka soldiers with Goi not to proceed any further with that plan. As a result, the group had to turn back. Goi then became sick and after being carried back to Angudri was arrested by Gbatala. Gbatala, it seems had been informed by Mondiri's friends that Goi was also planning to overthrow him.*

Meanwhile, Mondiri heard the news and hastened to Angudri with William Hassan, the ALF Chief of Staff". In a very confused situation, Ezboni was arrested on arrival but was soon released again by soldiers who had told Gbatala that they would not take part in any conspiracy against Ezboni. After release, Ezboni declared the coup over and prepared to return to Lomileŋwa GHQ to prepare for the Anyanya convention. The story however did not end up there. What had up to that point been a comedy of coups and counter coups, later ended tragically with the death of many people. Some of those who had earlier been arrested by Ezboni when he heard of the plot (Philip Angutowa, Francis Wajo) in Moru land and brought to Angudri escaped and went back to the Moru Headquarters at Ngiṛi", where they now plotted to oust Ezboni and drive out Lomileŋwa GHQ from Moru land "From there, a large force of Moru Anyanya set out for Lomileŋwa and fought several battles and as mentioned elsewhere. Ezboni escaped, Lomileŋwa was destroyed and with it ended the power of ALF in the west of the Nile".

Maj. Gen Scopas' Version

What McCall's narrative above gives is an overview or summary of the coup and the individuals involved. Retired Maj Gen Scopas Juma's version however is that, *"Paul Gbatala requested the transfer of Repent Sunday to his command at Maridi; and when he (Gbatala) was requested to move (without his forces) to Angudri in order to proceed to General Headquarters at Balgo Bindi, he therefore re-transferred Sunday from Maridi to Angudri and wanted him to follow him to Balgo Bindi. I was also transferred from Group D (Moru land) to Maridi*

Command Headquarters. But upon arrival (in Maridi), Gbatala immediately ordered me to proceed to Angudri, where he was with Sunday and Goyi (Ferdinand Goi, was an ex-seminarian a Balanda Bviri from Wau). Rev Fr. Ferdinand Goyi (not ordained) had received some help, assumed to have been given by some Verona Fathers and Goyi had staged an unsuccessful coup (against ALF/Ezboni). In the plot, Repent Sunday was expected to take the coup d'etat to Group D in Moru land. My name appeared as Adjutant General in the arrangement. (Because the coup had been exposed), Sunday stealthily went back to Moru land (Group D). My case was utterly refuted by many, including Gbatala himself. Ezboni was present in Angudri and was preparing to go to Lomileŋwa General Headquarters in Moru land. I was sandwiched in Mondiri's team to go immediately to Lomileŋwa Headquarters. So, we all went.

The journey from Angudri General Depot to Lomileŋwa is a day's hard travel (walk). As we entered Moru land, we learnt that troops at the General Headquarters had already clashed with those of Group D. (Ngiṛi Headquarters) and a few soldiers had been wounded, including Sadaraka Abisai, son of senior Lui dresser (Abisai)".

Morris' Version

The details of that epic journey of Ezboni from Angudri to Lomileŋwa GHQ were also provided by Morris Ägyili, who had been ordered to escort Ezboni. The story was that: *"We left with Ezboni and when we reached Tore Wande (in Moru land), we found out that the officers Philip Angotowa and Francis Wajo Biringi, who were arrested at Angudri and were to be escorted to the GHQ at Lomileŋwa, had escaped all, with the soldiers who were accompanying them; and their whereabouts were unknown.* (Note: Repent Sunday had by this time slipped out of Angudri and headed for Ngiṛi), *Under such uncertain and risky circumstance, I divided the soldiers who were accompanying us into two: one section of the soldiers was to escort Ezboni along the eastern bank of the rivers of Tore and Yei on to Lomileŋwa; and the other one was to be with me to go along the western bank of the rivers of Tore and Yei; and both groups were to meet in Lomileŋwa. My group followed the western bank and spent that night in the home of Head Scout Gabriel Pataki Dodo. The next day on our way, we met some soldiers (coming) from the GHQ and who were heading to Tore Wande. In response to my queries, they told us that they were ordered by Major William Hassan to go to Tore Wande under Sergeant Major Samuel Manyang. I enquired as to who Sergeant Major Manyang was, and they told me that he was an informer for the Arabs in Rumbek and had been arrested and sent to GHQ to be tried. That struck me as strange. So, I asked as to who released him and gave him a gun and the responsibility to lead GHQ solders to Tore Wande? They responded that it was William Hassan who gave the orders and was also the one who asked them to go to Tore Wande. Thereafter, the two parties rejoined and arrived at Lomileŋwa to find a very tense situation".*

The Fighting and the Fall of Lomileŋwa GHQ

Upon arrival, the situation and subsequent events leading to the fall of Lomileŋwa is better described by Scopas, quote *"The security situation in the General Headquarters and surrounding areas was very bad and ration (food) problem had worsened considerably. The natives were now running away from the General Headquarters areas towards enemy side, that is, the no man's land. This situation angered or at least displeased the Secretary for Defence (Ezboni). Soon upon arrival at the General Headquarters, and after briefing by the Chief of Staff (William Hassan), on the overall security situation, the Secretary of Defence Mr. Mondiri ordered a force to push away any forces of Goup D near to the General Headquarters back to their initial position. Ngiṛi had already deployed some of their forces as covering troops to their headquarters. The two forces met and an encounter battle ensued, where the Lomileŋwa (General Headquarters) troops were forced back to their positions, after offering serious resistance. Casualties including the wounded on both sides were very minor"*

Scopas' note continues, *"The relationship between Group D and Lomileŋwa General Headquarters continued to worsen. (Unfortunately,), no efforts were made for some form of peace conference or negotiation between Ngiṛi, the Group D Command Headquarters and the Anyanya General Headquarters. There was no intervention from nearby Commands; that is, the Central Equatoria or Maridi Commands. The Deputy C-in-C (Brig Paul Ali Gbatala) did not attempt any options for peace talks or military intervention. The B Command of Central Equatoria under Captain Philip Angotowa instead was sympathetic with Ngiṛi, but did not send any forces to their aid.*

The net security situation around the General Headquarters (had become) very bad and the relationship between Lomileŋwa and neighboring civilians (had) also become very bad. I had to go out with a small team to attempt to normalize the tension by persuading the people to remain calm and not to flee towards the roads. We had to go very far from the General Headquarters in order to meet the civilians. I even instructed the food patrols not to go after the people fleeing away and not to collect or take food from the granaries and houses that have been left behind".

The Attack and Destruction of Lomileŋwa GHQ

While Scopas was still out on the food mission from the GHQ, he says quote *"The second day, I heard heavy gunfire in the direction of the General Headquarters. I immediately decided to go back to the camp because the gunfire clearly indicated serious fighting. (At first), I reasoned that the enemy (Arab) forces were far away and could not have by passed us and attack the camp at our rear. (So), I guessed it should be probably an attack mounted by (the) Ngiṛi forces.*

The earlier battle of Ngiṛi covering troops with the detachment of General Headquarters had been used by Ngiṛi G-1's as reconnaissance force; and Ngiṛi commanders had consequently planned and now conducted a deliberate attack on Lomileŋwa. As we approached the camp, we found that all perimeter defences of the General Headquarters had already evacuated their positions and the situation around the camp was totally quiet and forlorn."

In other words, *"The Anyanya General Headquarters at Lomileŋwa had been attacked and defeated and the remaining forces had fled towards Nuni in Central Equatoria Command, under Morta Headquarters. We saw that there was no need for us to enter and inspect the deserted camp and so I followed the withdrawing forces to Nuni. We only had one gun for defence of the team and so we followed them on parallel axis, fearing being apprehended by Ngiṛi pursuing forces (forces in pursuit of the withdrawal). We, however, established contacts with the rear guard of the General Headquarter withdrawing forces and I was fully briefed on the overall situation. Casualties and the wounded were very minor and not as estimated by some writers, that is, of around 30."*

End of Ezboni's Dream

That destruction of Lomileŋwa GHQ marked the end of ALF Government (military), west of the Nile. On 22 January 1967, its Patron Fr. Saturnino was killed; and a little later its political leadership under Joseph Oduho east of the Nile also came to an end, as he was forced out by Brigadier Lazarus Mutek of Group B.

There have been wild allegations among some of the Moru local politicians as well as by some elements of the defunct Moru Anyanya to the effect that Ezboni brought Dinkas, especially one called Samuel Manyang, to fight the Moru people; and that Samuel Manyang, who eventually got killed by the Moru Anyanya, was the head of that Dinka group. Those stories as had been clarified in Morris Ägyili's submission, are not correct. According to Morris, Samuel Manyang was in Lomileŋwa as a prisoner to be tried for collaborating with the government. It was Captain William Hassan in the heat of things who released him and made him to command a small GHQ unit. Ezboni had nothing to do with him. Additionally, as is clear from the two eye witnesses, Ezboni was not directly responsible for initiating the fighting between the GHQ soldiers and the Moru Anyanya. His role, as will be elaborated in subsequent chapters, lies in his failure to enlighten the Moru Anyanya sufficiently to understand his goals.

The Unravelling and the Collapse of ALF

A closing of this Chapter on Ezboni's role in the Anyanya (Southern Sudan Resistance Movement) would be incomplete without mentioning the collapse of the ALF in its entirety. As had also been mentioned earlier, the ALF had scattered headquarters as follows: the Patron Fr. Saturnino was in Tul, its President Joseph Oduho was in Dito and its Army Headquarters, under Major General Taffeng Lodongi was in Lorifa (all in Latuka area). Its Minister of Defence, Ezboni Mondiri, was in Lomileŋwa (Moru area); and its Secretariat under Severino Fuli was in Loreze in Ma'di land.

The collapse of ALF began with the killing of the Patron Fr. Saturnino by Ugandan troops on 22 January 1967. That was followed by the collapse of the political leadership under President Joseph Oduho. How Oduho's leadership came collapse is well covered in Severino Fuli's book. That is, on his (Fuli's) return from the six-month mission tour with Ezboni in the western bank of River Nile, he found the east bank was in disarray. It was such that Fr Saturnino and Lagu were on one side and Joseph Oduho and Taffeng Lodongi were on the other. The relations between them was so bad that the two sides even engaged in some skirmishes. As a concerned nationalist, he Fuli single-handedly took it upon himself to organize and to convene a reconciliation meeting for all in Eastern Equatoria. The meeting was held on 13-15 March 1967 at Imokoru and it was very successful. As a result the civil administration was revitalized and relationships greatly improved.

However, one of the resolutions of the meeting was the formation of a Mobile Unit, an elite force under Chief of Staff Joseph Lagu for rapid response purposes. The Unit was to take and incorporate the best soldiers from all commands in Eastern Equatoria. In effecting it, both General Taffeng and Brigadier Lazarus Mutek lost some of their best soldiers and armaments. That, coupled with the non-supply of arms and ammunition by the political leadership, made both of them to be angry with Oduho. They accused him of conniving with Lagu to undermine them by taking away their best soldiers. They therefore felt that Oduho was a liability and requested him to leave and never to return. Consequently, Oduho left the Movement and went to Uganda never to resurface. In that way, the political headquarters of the ALF was brought down by the Anyanya just as it subsequently happened to its military headquarters at Lomileŋwa under Eiboni. So, with both Oduho and Ezboni gone, courtesy of the Anyanya, ALF came to an end.

CHAPTER X: ANALYSIS AND REASONS FOR THE COUP

Persons Involved in the Coup

In the light of the above narratives by McCall, Scopas Juma and Morris Ägyili, it is possible to identify individuals who were involved in the coup and the roles they played in the saga. These include:

1. Paul Ali Gbatala

He had always been a Deputy to Taffeng and in charge of Group A. He either was complicit in the coup or his ignorance was used by the coup plotters, especially by Ferdinand Goi. He probably was not too well disposed towards Ezboni. As may be recalled, in the Ibba Meeting (21- 22 September 1966), he was unenthusiastic about ALF and the New Policy Program, even when he was told that he still was the deputy to Taffeng. Instead, he warned Ezboni about the politicians who always were letting down the Southern people and also warned him about communism. The warning about communism was a surprise, coming as it did from a person of his level of understanding. Because, as was the case in those days, Southerners generally were more concerned about freeing themselves from Northern domination than care about global ideologies like communism. As the case was, Ali Gbatala at that time had been baptized and become a Christian. So, he might have either acquired the anti- communist feeling from the missionaries in Congo; or the idea was put in his mind by ex-seminarian Goi.

Secondly, Gbatala had been close to Jackson Garaŋwa. The latter used to visit and spend long time with him. So, it is possible that Jackson transferred his antipathy towards Ezboni to Gbatala. Thirdly, Gbatala's actions, just before the coup, would implicate him in the plot. It was no coincidence that soon after executing the action against Jackson's camp in Kedi'ba on instructions from Ezboni; and disagreeing with him, that Gbatala requested Repent Sunday first to go to his base in Maridi; then ordered him to go to Angudri where he (Repent Sunday) met and connived with Goi and Camillo to stage the coup. Fourthly, when the coup had been worked out, it was Gbatala who signed the declaration of the overthrow of Ezboni and the ALF government. However, when he found that the plot had been leaked to Ezboni, he quickly turned around and arrested Goi for the abortive coup. Also, in a quick turn-around to distance himself from the coup and be seen as supportive of Ezboni, he called Morris from Maridi area and asked him to accompany Ezboni back to Lomileŋwa GHQ after the coup had collapsed. In the light of his actions, like signing the declaration of the coup and then arresting the coup leader Goi, Ali Gbatala's role in the whole affair could at best be described as dubious.

2. Ferdinand Goi

He was a Balanda Bviri from Baggari near Wau and who left the seminary in Milan Italy in 1962 and joined the Anyanya in Wau area. He was the main architect and leader of the coup. A politically very ambitious person who, when he joined the Anyanya in Western Bahr El Ghazal, was instrumental in the overthrow of the leader and founder of the Anyanya, Filberto Ucini. Sometime after that, he went to Congo and obtained some funds from some Catholic priests and came to Angudri. McCall alleges that it is through Goi that some members of the Catholic clergy are accused of being behind the attempt to remove ALF, especially Ezboni, from leadership of the Southern Resistance Movement. Their support to Goi was based on the grounds that Ezboni was a communist (see latter story).

In Angudri, Goi found common cause with Repent Sunday and Camillo Odongi to mount the coup. The trio succeeded to convince Gbatala to sign the document declaring the overthrow of the ALF. In the plot, Goi was to lead the operation to oust Ezboni and take control of the Lomileŋwa GHQ. Unfortunately, as mentioned earlier, the plot was discovered and it came to the notice of Ezboni at Lomileŋwa, where he hurried to Angudri to arrest it. Upon arrival, he was briefly arrested but promptly released, since the ordinary soldiers refused to go along with the coup. In the light of that, Ali Gbatala arrested Goi but Repent Sunday managed to slip away to Ngiṛi in Moru land.

3. Repent Sunday

He was one of the key coup plotters. Much has already been explained about the poor relations between Repent Sunday and Ezboni. Since Ezboni joined the Anyanya in May 1965, Repent Sunday had usually been away for extended periods of time. At one time, he was in the general area of Yei and Congo searching for weapons for the group. Hence, some of the Ezboni-initiated operations like the attack on Jambo police post were done in his absence. It is quite likely that he did not like Ezboni's dabbling in military matters. It is also likely that he might have come into contact with Ezboni's political rivals like Ezboni Jo'di, who could be considering Ezboni as a Johnny-come-lately, in taking the leadership of the Moru Anyanya. In fact, as already mentioned earlier, Fuli alleges that his antipathy towards Ezboni might have been induced Elisapana Käbi Mulla and/or Ezboni Jo'di.

Repent also did not like the operation he led against the Kedi'ba camp which Ezboni had ordered him to execute. For that reason, he arrested Ezboni together with Aggrey and Morris and sent them to Angudri. Lastly, like the rest of the Moru Anyanya, Repent Sunday could have been angry with Ezboni for bringing the GHQ in Moru land without consulting them. On those grounds, when Ali Gbatala transferred him to Maridi and eventually to Angudri, he found common cause with Goi and Camillo and he became one of the leaders of the coup. And as already mentioned, when he came to be aware that the plot had been discovered and Ezboni had arrived at Angudri, he slipped secretly and came to Ngiri. There he joined hands with Francis Wajo and Philip Angotowa in their determination to dislodge Lomileŋwa GHQ, together with Ezboni from the area.

4. Camillo Odongi

He was another key coup plotter. He was one of the assistants (runners) of late Fr. Saturnino in Congo and possibly through the Catholic connection must have known Ferdinand Goi. It is possible that he was recruited into the plot by Goi. However, his real interest in removing ALF and Ezboni remains unknown. But he could have done so in sympathy with his fellow Latuka officers, particularly Brigadier Lazarus Mutek in the east, who had by then deposed and sent ALF President Joseph Oduho away to Uganda.

5. Francis Wajo and Philip Angotowa

They were officers of the Moru Anyanya at Ngiṛi and their reasons for disagreement with Ezboni is not exactly known. They might also have been disappointed with him for bringing the Anyanya GHQ into their (Group D) area without sufficiently enlightening them. They most likely supported Repent Sunday's arrest of Ezboni in early 1966. It is however difficult to tell whether they were part of the conspiracy that was planned and led by Goi against ALF and Ezboni. Knowing that they were opposed to him after learning about the coup in Angudri, Ezboni had them arrested. They were taken to Angudri for onward transfer to the GHQ at Lomileŋwa for trial. But while they were being taken from Angudri under guard to GHQ at Lomileŋwa for trial, they convinced the soldiers who were guarding them and escaped back to Ngiṛi. They were soon joined by Repent Sunday and they now were ready to launch the offensive against Ezboni's base, the Lomileŋwa GHQ.

Underlying Causes for the Coup
Introductory Remarks

In the preceding paragraphs, we have identified the coup leaders and very briefly had outlined the probable motives for their conducting the coup against Ezboni, Lomileŋwa GHQ and ALF in general. In the subsequent paragraphs, we will attempt to gain insight into the underlying reasons for the coup. But first some background information is necessary.

While Ezboni was busy working on building of national institutions, notably the army and civil administration, unknown to him two problems developed in his backyard: The first one concerned him as the politico-military leader of the Moru Anyanya; and the second one concerned his being the Secretary of Defence for ALF. Though the two were different and did not occur at the same time, they were in some cases interconnected, through the involvement of some of the perpetrators in both affairs. For example, Repent Sunday who led the rebellion against Ezboni among the Moru Anyanya, was also one of the conspirators against ALF and Ezboni, together with Ferdinand Goi and Camillo Odongi.

As the case was, the ouster eventually ruined Ezboni's goal of building an effective Anyanya fighting force, with a national composition and outlook. Those reasons, as put down here, were extracted from several sources: Severino Fuli's book and McCall's book; articles by Lt Gen. Scopas Juma and Morris Agyili; and those were buttressed with interviews with John Russie, Scopas Juma, Morris Ägyili and many others. Unfortunately, at the time of writing, the writer was unable to reach Repent Sunday and Jackson Garaŋwa, to get their views of those events. Other reasons for the coup were obtained from the writer's conversations with Ezboni himself as well as from the writer's personal observations and analysis of the situations that obtained in those days. In doing that, we first will list those reasons for which Ezboni was ousted by the Moru Anyanya, as their politico-military leader and within that, we will look at Ezboni's own personal failings. Subsequently we will look at the plausibility and reasons for the involvement of some Catholic clergymen in the coup.

Reasons Arising from Ezboni's Difficulties with the Local Anyanya Leaders

1. Differences in the Level of Education and Understanding

This indeed is the main cause of the difference between Ezboni and the Moru Anyanya leaders. The differences in level of education, knowledge, intellect, political and global understanding of what is at stake in the Southern struggle was at main root cause of the difference between Ezboni and the local Anyanya leaders, majority of whom hardly went beyond intermediate level of education. In politics of the struggle, many of them had difficulties in contextualizing the struggle in the national content as opposed to the parochial and tribal interests. Needless to underscore that, Ezboni's experience, knowledge and exposure to the politics of the Sudan was unmatched by those who were opposing him. Hence, there was a very wide chasm between his views and theirs. Whereas, Ezboni was operating at the higher national level, the local Anyanya, just like the other local Anyanya groups elsewhere in Southern Sudan, were operating at local tribal levels. So this is and was at the root cause of

Ezboni's differences with the local Anyanya. As the Gospel of St Luke 4:24 says, usually prophets are not respected in their home areas

2. Interfering with Military Affairs and Structures

As the case was, the Anyanya all over the then Southern Sudan were very wary of politicians and they guarded their military affairs very jealously. As may be recalled, one of the points underlined by Paul Ali Gbatala to Ezboni in the Ibba Meeting of September 1966 was, quote. *"the Anyanya under command of Maj General Emidio Taffeng are to be left alone by the politicians"*. In the Moru Anyanya, however, when Ezboni arrived in Moru land, out of respect for him, they allowed him to dabble in their military affairs. For example, Ezboni planned and directed the attack on the police post at Jambo in June 1965. He also planned the attempt to capture Mundri in October of the same year. According to Lt. General Scopas, *Ezboni "tried to use his position of Secretary of Defence and functions to interfere in Anyanya activities, such as promoting and transferring officers and even to take command of operations"*. The officer corps thus strongly resented this to the extent that even his confidant Morris Ägyili, after the Mundri fiasco, advised him to leave military matters and join the other politicians in East Africa, where he would be most useful. This certainly was one of the contributory factors for the Moru Anyanya officers' antipathy towards Ezboni.

The Attempt to Forcefully Integrate the Kedi'ba Anyanya

Ezboni's efforts to unite the two groups of the Moru Anyanya were some of the factors that contributed to the fall out between him and the local Anyanya. As is known, the split predated his arrival. His genuine effort to achieve reintegration was frustrated by the obstinacy and antics of Jackson Garaŋwa, who succeeded to twist the issue as if it were a Miza versus Kädiro affair. Ezboni's order to bring the Kedi'ba group under his fold by use of force only brought him more resentment to the extent that, immediately after the military operation, he was arrested by Repent Sunday, beaten and sent to Angudri to be tried.

3. Differences with Jackson Garaŋwa

The reasons for the differences between Ezboni and Jackson Garaŋwa have been explained elsewhere and are much related to the reasons outlined in the above paragraph. Suffice to reiterate here that differences in the level of education and of the wide gap between the political and national goals of the struggle underscored the differences between them. From his lower level of understanding and operation, Jackson was able to twist and convince some elements of the Kädiro Section that Ezboni, as a Miza was against them- something that was absolutely baseless.

Differences with Repent Sunday

This has also been explained severally elsewhere. Repent's resentment to Ezboni could have emanated either from Ezboni's meddling in military affairs (see below); or, according to Fuli, from coming under the influence of Ezboni's political rivals, Ezboni Jo'di and Elisapana Käbi. On that ground, Sunday first arrested Ezboni and later he readily joined Goi's plot to overthrow Ezboni and the ALF government.

4. Political Rivals

As may be recalled, Ezboni Mondiri and Ezboni Jo'di were rivals in the 1958 general elections, which Ezboni Mondiri won. However, when the Southern Resistance Movement began, Ezboni Jo'di was the first leading Moru politician to join it. Thus, he was one of the key persons in the establishment of the Moru Anyanya. But in April 1965, Ezboni Mondiri arrived in Moru land and in a short time, was in charge of the Moru Anyanya to the chagrin of Ezboni Jo'di. So it is quite likely that, he influenced and/or used Repent Sunday, possibly together with Elisapana, to get at Ezboni. As already mentioned above, Fuli in his book alleges that there was such a conspiracy.

5. Antipathy Towards Lomileŋwa GHQ

As mentioned in the previous chapters, Ezboni as the Minister of Defence of ALF, toured and explained the New Policy Program thoroughly to the other Anyanya groups, including the idea of a single and united Anyanya command structure. He, however, did not do the same in Moru people and/or to the Moru Anyanya group, perhaps, on the assumption that they would follow him anyway. So, because he did not sensitize and consult the Moru people and especially the local Anyanya sufficiently about the location of the GHQ at Lomileŋwa in what they considered as their area of responsibility, they took a resentment to the presence of the GHQ right from its inception. Additionally, with undefined responsibilities and *modus operandi* in the same area, a hostile relationship inevitably was bound to arise between the Moru Anyanya at Ngiṛi and the GHQ at Lomileŋwa. The local Anyanya at Ngiṛi were afraid that they could be subsumed in their own land by the GHQ. This antipathy was shared by the civilian population, who refused to supply food to the GHQ. So, it was only a matter of time that the bad relationship would break out into violent confrontations between Ngiṛi and the GHQ. Additionally, as it was the case, there were several non-Moru soldiers in the GHQ. They were there for different reasons: some were sent by their commands to the GHQ for integration; others were on their way to Congo to purchase arms; yet more others were sent to GHQ for detention and/or trial because of mistakes (usually government informers) they had allegedly committed in their home commands.

With such varied and dubious backgrounds, some of those soldiers were misbehaving towards the civilians, especially during food collection missions. They also were picking up quarrels with the local Anyanya of Group D. Hence, both the local Anyanya and civilians resented them and they blamed Ezboni for bringing those soldiers into their area and who were now harassing them.

Reasons Attributable to Ezboni's Own Failings
1. Unawareness

Perhaps because Ezboni was too much absorbed in realizing his national dreams to the extent that he either forgot his constituents, the people and Moru Anyanya, or had taken them for granted. He, thus, might not have been aware of the growing resentment against him. Those failings could be seen in the following: firstly, Ezboni should have appreciated the level of understanding of the people he was dealing with. He should have adopted a more educative approach on issues such as: enlightening them, especially as to why they were fighting. He should have pointed out the importance of integration of the forces for the achievement of goals of the struggle. He should have elucidated national *vis a vis* the local or tribal aspects of the struggle and which, in effect, were not mutually exclusive. Secondly, Ezboni appeared not to have gauged the feelings of the people. According to Major General Scopas Juma, he (Ezboni) *"thought it was a right and superior order to establish the General Headquarters at Lomileŋwa and hence no need to request the views of the citizens and the (*local*) Anyanya group there. He therefore considered the resentment of Group D as mere insubordination and gross disobedience. He assumed that it was complete violation of orders of the legitimate Secretary for Defence and should be addressed even by use of force"*. Whereas, Ezboni was consummated in the bigger picture, the struggle for the liberation of Southern Sudan.

2. Failure to Sensitize the Moru Anyanya and Civilians about the New Policy

As already mentioned above, in his tour with Severino Fuli, Ezboni did not explain the changes that had taken place at the leadership of the Movement as well as of the New Policy Program to the Moru Anyanya and people, as he had done elsewhere. As may be recalled, in those parts, he ensured that the Anyanya leadership, civil administrators and chiefs were present in those meetings to hear of the changes. Furthermore, in their mission, they did not go to all parts of the Moru area. Thus, the Moru Anyanya and civilians were not fully aware of the New Policy Program.

3. Absence of a Modus Operandi Between GHQ and the Local Anyanya

When two forces are deployed in the same area, invariably relationships and limits of operations must be clearly defined between them so that misunderstanding would not occur. This, as could be seen, was not done. There was thus no *modus operandi* on how the two forces of the GHQ at Lomileŋwa and Ngiṟi were to exercise authority in the same area administratively and militarily. That undefined situation was the cause of the misunderstanding and inevitably the clashes. So, given the fact that the Anyanya organization all over the South was tribally based, the Moru Anyanya felt that their tribal area was their sole area of operation. They therefore came to see the General Headquarter troops as usurping powers over the area in which they were to reign supreme. That created great resentment amongst them towards the General Headquarters and they therefore accused Ezboni of bringing outsiders to operate in their home area.

On the part of the civilians, they found themselves between two authorities, Ngiṟi and Lomileŋwa, particularly as regards contribution of food and supply of labor to the two camps. The burden was particularly heavy on the women who had to grind grains for the two camps, since there were no grinding mills during that time. They particularly resented grinding grains for the Lomileŋwa group, which they considered alien. Furthermore, both the civilians and the Moru Anyanya resented officers of the GHQ also exercising authority over their Chiefs and Head Scouts. Hence, many people blamed Ezboni for having brought what they see as foreigners to their area to bother them.

Reasons Traceable to External Conspiracy
Foreign Instigation

McCall in his manuscript and book implicates the hands of the Catholic fathers (Church) in the overthrow of Ezboni on the grounds that he was a communist. As had been explained earlier, the allegation that Ezboni and the other Southern students in the University of Khartoum were communists emanated from their student days in the university, when in the student politics, the Southern students allied themselves with the liberals, socialists and communists. In his autobiography Hilary Logali, a contemporary of Ezboni, says that in the student politics in the university they, the Southern students, usually allied themselves with the left-wing socialists, communists and liberals, *vis a vis* the right-wing traditional political parties and Moslem Brothers in the North. That alliance was misinterpreted by the church missionaries at that time that Southern students in the university had all become communists. It was this false allegation that had persisted in missionary circles and it appears to have been widely circulated, as evidenced by the warning of Paul Ali Gbatala, then a recent Muslim convert to Catholicism, in the Ibba Meeting in September 1966. As will be seen later, this same allegation was used to exclude Ezboni from attending the Second National Convention at Angudri in July 1967.

In view of the above, McCall's allegation of Catholic Church involvement was based on the fact that, when the Southern Resistance Movement began, it was primarily backed by the Catholic Church and they used to fund it through its Patron, Fr. Saturnino Ohure. Therefore, through this, they had very significant influence on the movement. He surmises that, when Fr. Saturnino was killed by Ugandan troops on 22 January 1967, their link to the Movement was lost. It is, therefore, possible that, with Joseph Oduho as President and Ezboni being as the most powerful person in ALF, they feared that the Movement was now about to pass into the communist world through Ezboni; and so he would have to be removed. That was why some Catholic clergy in Congo gave money to Ferdinand Goi, the master-mind of the coup, to effect Ezboni's removal from the Movement.

Reasons Emanating from Anyanya Mistrust of Politicians

Nature of the Anyanya

In his book McCall pointed out to several instances of how the Anyanya had always regarded politicians and intellectuals with a mixture of suspicion, jealousy and sometimes outright hostility. He went on to conclude that, quote"*This is a very diffcult body to handle. If a politician claims that he has the loyalty of the Anyanya in his area, such a politician is deceiving himself*". In their behavior, they had no qualms about arresting and humiliating any political leadership of the Movement. For example, Ezboni Mondiri was tied up and beaten on the orders of Repent Sunday; in May/June 1967, ALF President Joseph Oduho was unceremoniously expelled and ordered never to return by Brig Lazarus Mutek and Major General Taffeng Lodongi; and in December 1966, Severino Fuli was detained in a hut for several days by Major General Taffeng Lodongi. Those instances aptly capture and underline the difficulty of working with the Anyanya. Furthermore, though at various levels and intensity all over the country, the ordinary civilians fared no better in the hands of the Anyanya. For example, in Chapter VI, we read about the atrocities committed by the Moru Anyanya towards the civilians until the arrival of Ezboni in April 1965.

On the other hand, Maj Gen PSC Scopas Juma, a former Anyanya officer, in his article states that in the relationship with civilians the Anyanya was initially harsh because they, the Anyanya, wanted to stamp their authority but he claims that those excesses were later abandoned and that they lived in harmony with the civilians. Scopas disagreed with the view in McCall's book that '*the Anyanya were a difcult body to handle*,' stating that the Anyanya were "*a decisive group, tolerant, courageous and nationalistic*". He also disagreed with the view that the Anyanya did not like educated persons and politicians, stating that "*the early Anyanya needed the presence of politicians and educated people for political evaluation of the on- going war, activities of the Anyanya in other areas, the general policy of enemy-government and the stance of the neighboring countries.....*". He went on to state that the Anyanya needed the politicians for advice but added the caveat that they "*did not tolerate politicians who act as opponents*". Nonetheless, this view shows the ambivalence with which the Anyanya regarded the politicians.

CHAPTER XI:
THE MOVEMENT AFTER THE COLLAPSE OF THE AZANIA LIBERATION FRONT

Aggrey Jaden's Initiative for Reconciliation and Restoration of the Movement

To the Rescue

The information here is based on McCall's book as well as from manuscripts by Major General Scopas Juma Kamonde and Morris Ägyili Ori Lo'dio and interviews with some of those who were witnesses to those occurrences. It was that, when the fighting that eventually led to the fall of Lomileŋwa GHQ was taking place, Aggrey Jaden was in his home area of Yondoru in Pojulu area and not too far from Lomileŋwa. At that time, he was the Chairman of the Central Equatoria Defence Council. Aggrey was saddened by what he heard regarding the destruction of GHQ in Lomileŋwa. He also was saddened by the fact that with Oduho and Ezboni gone, ALF had collapsed and there was now no Southern Resistance Movement.

Being the nationalist he was, he decided to embark on reconciliation of the two sides, the Moru Anyanya and the GHQ (Ezboni). He therefore took a tour up to the Moru area and met several Pojulu and Moru chiefs. In his meetings, the plea of the chiefs for reconciliation reinforced his conviction for a general reconciliation but particularly for restoring the Movement through a convention of the people. He returned and went to Aba in Congo to mobilize the other political leaders who were residing in Congo, such as Elia Lupe, Camillo Dhol, Daniel Jumi, Ezboni Jo'di, Eliaba Surur and many more others for the convention. Aggrey's idea for holding the convention was to reconcile and reconstitute a new political leadership. His initiative received an overwhelming support from all those who heard about it. According to Major Gen. Scopas Juma, Aggrey tasked him to move around on a bicycle to carry the message to the Southern leaders in Sudan and Congo and also to publicise the date and venue of the Second Convention in Angudri.

The Angudri Convention and the Southern Sudan Provisional Government (SSPG)
Resolutions of the Convention

It is to be mentioned that this was to be the second convention held by Southerners to choose a political leadership for their Movement. The first one was held in Uganda on 30th September 1964, when Aggrey was elected as the President of SANU.

The Convention was duly held on 18 August (historic day)

1967 and it was attended by 300 delegates, 100 from each of the three provinces. Several resolutions were reached and they generally were:

1. *The hostility between Group D (Moru Anyanya at Ngiri) GHQ troops should be abandoned and good relations restored;*
2. *The GHQ should move to Central Equatoria at Balgo Bindi, later Bungu;*
3. *The Anyanya should now be renamed Anyanya National Armed Forces (ANAF) and its leadership should remain the same: Emidio Taffeng, Commander in-Chief; Paul Ali Gbatala, Deputy Commander in- Chief; and Joseph Lagu as Chief of Staff;*
4. *A provisional government should be formed instead of a political party (Aggrey's idea) and the government should be based inside the Sudan.*

Following those resolutions, Aggrey Jaden was elected as the President of the Southern Sudan Provisional Government, (SSPG) with Camillo Dhol as the Vice President, and Aggrey proceeded to form the cabinet.

Ezboni Excluded from the Convention

Although Ezboni was in Angudri, he was excluded from attending the Convention that led to the formation of the SSPG under Aggrey. Two reasons could be adduced as to why he was not invited to attend. Firstly, Ferdinand Goi was one of the key organizers of the Convention. Being the protégé of some influential Catholic priests, it is most likely that he was the one who campaigned for Ezboni's exclusion on grounds that he, Ezboni, was a communist. Secondly, Ezboni could also have been excluded from the Convention as well as in emerging new dispensation in order to placate the Moru Anyanya, who were still demanding for Ezboni to be handed over to them for trial, so that they could agree to be integrated into the new ANAF command structure.

Arrest and Detention

According to Morris, after spending a month in Angudri, one day, *"it was a surprise to us to see that Mr. Ezboni Jo'di, a politician, who resides at Faraje District of Democratic Republic of Congo was brought to Angudri Depot under arrest and we did not know the reason of his arrest. In a few days' time, the Defence Minister Ezboni Mondiri Gwonza, Major William Hassan, Major Aggrey Andago, and myself were all arrested and put under detention and we did not know the reason why we were arrested. Among us (the senior officers in the GHQ) the person who were not arrested were Captain Peter Cirillo, a Bari by tribe, and Captain Emmanuel Abur, a Dinka, who had earlier already left for Isiro, where some Dinka Anyanya soldiers were (residing).*

In a few days' time, we were moved to from Angudri, together with all of our Anyanya Army HQs staff of Lomileŋwa (Morolanyi) to a certain Anyanya camp between Yei District and Aba Sub-District of Democratic Republic of Congo. On arrival in that camp, we noticed that Captain Peter Cirillo had been promoted to the rank of Major and Commander of the Anyanya Army Hqs".

According to McCall, the reason for Ezboni's detention was that he was a communist, because of a draft letter found in his possession, requesting assistance from China. McCall in his assessment described that reason of no serious consequence, since the assistance could have helped the Southerners in their dire need for weapons; but which he said without doubt went against *"their mission-influenced background and ideology"*.

Last Ditch Effort to Get Ezboni

While Ezboni was in detention a Moru Anyanya delegation headed by Elisapana Mulla arrived at Angudri and made a request to Aggrey and SSPG to handover Ezboni and his two aids to them so as to be tried for having caused the fight between them and the GHQ in Lomileŋwa. But the request was refused on the grounds that more time was still needed to study the case. Moreover, they were told to produce concrete evidence of the crimes allegedly committed by Ezboni. With this, the Moru Anyanya gave up the chase of Ezboni and here ended a sad and shameful episode in the history of the Moru people and which confirmed the story in St Luke Chapter 4 verse 24, that a prophet is not respected in his own home.

Illness and Escape

According to Ezboni his time in detention in that camp was another of his worst times in the Movement. Because, he didn't see the reason for his detention and, worst still, by his very own colleagues. He thus became disillusioned and depressed. Regarding his situation, Morris had this to say, *'after a few days' time, the Defence Minister Ezboni Mondiri Gwonza developed some illness and he asked permission to from Major Peter Cirillo to go to the hospital at Aba for treatment and Major Peter Cirillo approved it and he was accompanied (escorted) to Aba Hospital for treatment'.* On their way to Aba, Ezboni and escort passed through SSPG Headquarters on 14 March 1968, where Severino Fuli was. Fuli in his book says that he was astonished to see him (Ezboni) after 17 months, looking haggard and tired. He was asked to rest but he declined and only drank water and left. When Fuli asked as to what happened, one of his aides whispered that, quote: *"the Anyanya of Moru, engineered by Governor Elisapana Mulla and Ezboni Jo'di (his cousin) stormed and overran the Lomileŋwa Anyanya General Headquarters"*. From Aba in Congo, Ezboni possibly convinced his escort to let him cross over into Uganda. This was Ezboni's second escape from capture. As may be recalled, in 1958, he escaped from the policemen at Mundri.

Back in the detention camp, and also according to Morris, after the departure and escape of *"the Defence Minister Ezboni Mondiri Gwonza, to Aba Sub- District for treatment, things began changing against us in detention. Bad conspiracy was going on for our destruction, and that was because news came to the camp that the Defence Minister Ezboni Mondiri Gwonza had escaped from Aba to Uganda and that Major Peter Cirillo was trying his very best to do something bad to us as revenge because Ezboni had escaped. After examining carefully the attitude of Major Peter Cirillo and his gang who were trying to harm us for no reason, we set and thought to do something to save our own lives; and we decided to escape from the prison. But before we did that, we convinced the guard who was guarding us and when we knew that he had completely consented to our idea, we made off and escaped from the prison by night to Aba the Sub-District of the Democratic Republic of Congo and settled there as refugees. Our guard who escaped with us was called Captain Peter, a Dinka by tribe from Renk".*

So here it can be said that, except for Peter Cirillo, ended the fate of the senior officers of the Anyanya GHQ at Lomileŋwa that operated under the administration of the ALF President, Joseph Oduho Haworu.

Out of the Movement

Following his escape into Uganda, Ezboni travelled to Kampala and then to Jinja, where he stayed with a distant relative. With nothing to do, Ezboni passed his time fishing in the Lake with a line. After sometime, he took up a teaching job in Bombo Secondary School. During this period, he made no contacts with the Southern Resistance Movement. He toyed with the idea of forming a political party Sudan Azanian Party of East Africa but did not put much effort to practicalize it. His main companions were Stephen Lam and Alphonse Malek Pajokdit; otherwise, he was not active in politics. It was only in 1971, three years later, that he re-entered Southern politics again when, because of his known southern nationalistic stand, stature, integrity, unwavering and uncompromising stance towards the North, that he was recalled by General Joseph Lagu to lead the South Sudan Liberation Movement (SSLM) delegation to the Addis Ababa peace talks with the Sudan Government.

CHAPTER XII
THE SOUTHERN SUDAN PROVISIONAL GOVERNMENT (SSPG)

Programs and Activities of the SSPG

Going back to Chapter XI, we read that the Angudri National Convention was held and from it, several key resolutions were passed: Aggrey Jaden was elected as the President of the SSPG; he formed the cabinet; and thereafter he laid out the programs for his government. All those were done while Ezboni was still under detention. Thereafter, Aggrey called a meeting of the cabinet to operationalize the resolutions of the Convention. Interestingly, many of those programs were lifted from Ezboni's New Program for the ALF Government which he presented in meeting in Tul (see Chapter VIII) in the Imatong Mountains.

On the military front and similar to Ezboni's ideas, the core of the policy was integration and unifying the Anyanya under one command structure from top to the bottom, instead of the Anyanya being a multi-headed monster it had been. In that, the officers and ranks were to be rotated out of their home areas and sent to work in other districts and provinces; and that the buying of was to be centralized in the Ministry of Defence under Akwot Atem, deputized by Ferdinand Goi. On the diplomatic front, Serafino Wani Swaka was appointed to be the SSPG representative in Kampala to liaise with foreign envoys. In fact, this was the time when contacts began with Israel. On the administrative front, the number of Regions or Provinces was increased from Ezboni's seven to nine; that is, three per the three larger Provinces of Equatoria, Upper Nile and Bahr El Ghazal.

An interesting development in this reorganization of the provinces was that the Moru area (Amadi/Mundri) was placed in Central Equatoria, together with Juba and Yei. According to McCall, that came about as a result of the Zande delegation in the conference maintaining *"that the territory covered by Yambio and Maridi Districts was too large to be encompassed within one single administrative region. It was therefore decided that the Amadi Sub- District would be transferred from Western to Central Equatoria"*. The news of being placed in Central Equatoria was received with consternation in Moru area. The reason for the anger was because Amadi (Mundri) and Maridi have always administratively been one district since the Condominium era in the early 1930s. Moreover, the peoples of Amadi (Avokaya, Morokodo, Moru Wa'di) were also found in Maridi; and additionally they are very much more related ethnically, linguistically and culturally to Maridi people than to the Bari speakers of Central Equatoria.

In view of that, in January 1968, the Moru Anyanya sent a delegation to Angudri, headed by Elisapana Käbi Mulla[15] to express their objection to being placed in Central Equatoria. They argued that ever since the condominium government rule, their area had always been together with Maridi. But this protest was not honored. Hence, the Moru people refused to be in Central Equatoria and the area remained outside the SSPG administration.

Similarly, because of that, the Moru Anyanya (Group D) refused to be part of the Group B of Central Equaoria and chose to stand alone. However, Jackson Garaŋwa did send 30-40 soldiers to the ANAF. This situation obtained until when Joseph Lagu took over as the overall commander of the Anyanya and for logistic purposes, he created a Special Unit out of the Moru Anyanya, under Major Repent Sunday. That Special Unit directly answerable to him.

Turmoil in the SSPG

Aggrey Disappears from the Scene

Under President Aggrey, very many positive developments were put under way. The integration of the army was begun by sending military missions to the provinces. Those military missions were commanded by officers who were from another province to ensure integration. Civil administration had been set up and diplomatic contacts had been established with foreign countries. McCall assessed that, had Aggrey stayed a little longer,

---

15   It was this same delegation that had requested SSPG to hand Ezboni over to them but, as mentioned, the request was refused.

the Southern Movement would have achieved something. But suddenly Aggrey disappeared from the scene and went to Uganda. Nobody knew why. Many people, including Gordon Mourtat, the Foreign Minister wrote to him to come back but he did not respond. Gordon Mourtat even went up to Uganda to persuade him to come back but to no avail. In later years, he, Aggrey, told McCall that he simply was discouraged by the enormity of what needed to be done, in view of the formidable resistance to change on the ground. McCall surmises that the reason could have been due to his inability to reshuffle the cabinet as he would have wanted it; and/or due to the usual Equatoria/Dinka rivalries.

On the other hand, Fuli considered that it was due *to "a misunderstanding between Aggrey Jaden, who was pursuing contacts in Nairobi and his Foreign Minster Gordon Mourtat, who accused President Aggrey of being weak because Aggrey had allowed Joseph Lagu to work independently of the Government. Gordon then told Aggrey to report immediately to the headquarters at Bungu. When Aggrey failed to turn up, Gordon decided to remove him from the Presidency; and using some mock elections, he established what he called the Nile State and declared himself the President of the Nile Provisional Government, with Camillo Dhol as the Vice President".*

The Nile Provisional Government (NPG)

The takeover by Gordon Mourtat sparked differences that led to fighting. Many officers and rank and file of the Anyanya soldiers, especially from Equatoria, did not like the coup against Aggrey. So, many of them escaped from the main Headquarters at

Bungu to Morta, Headquarters of the Central Equatoria Command, among those who escaped was Frederick Magot Daŋgoro. In Morta, the officers and the C-in- C Emidio Taffeng, decided that the military (Anyanya) should take over, since the politicians had consistently failed to lead the struggle. Taffeng therefore sent a force to Bungu to depose the NPG and for the military to take over. Fighting ensued and the leaders of NPG fled Bungu to Balgo Bindi; and by this, the brief life of NPG came to an end. On 15 September 1969, a new military government called Anyidi Provisional Government was set up under General Emidio Taffeng Lodongi.

The Anyidi Provisional Government (APG)

The Anyidi Provisional Government comprised of Emidio Taffeng, President; Aggrey Jaden Foreign Affairs; Eliaba Surur, Finance and Administration; Frederick Magot, Chief of Staff; and Serafino Wani Swaka, a member of the cabinet without portfolio. However the APG did not last for long nor did it have time to initiate policies and/or programs. Soon Joseph Lagu moved and took it over and transformed it into a full military junta with a military High Command

Anyanya Military High Command and Government

The High Command was constituted of:

Gen Joseph Lagu	Major General and Commander in Chief, Leader SSLM
Brig Samuel Abu John	Brigadier and Deputy Commander
Brig Frederick Magot Daŋgoro	Equatoria Brigade
Brig. Emmanuel Abur	Bahr El Ghazal Brigade
Brig Joseph Akoun	Upper Nile Brigade

Thereafter the High Command formed its political wing, the 'Southern Sudan Liberation Movement' (SSLM) and Civil Departments of the Government were established for Foreign Affairs, Education, Health, Police Administration and Judiciary. With a better structure, support began to flow, notably from Israel. An air field was established at Owing-ki- Bul and Israel began to train the Anyanya offiers.

CHAPTER XIII:
THE DAWNING AND REALIZATION OF THE PEACE AGREEMENT

Lagu was now in full control of the Southern Resistance Movement. The Anyanya was now better structured and the Zande Anyanya that used to operate independently was now fully incorporated into the main Anyanya body. Consequently, with resources from the Israelis the Anyanya was fighting more effectively.

Circumstances and Events that Promoted the March to Peace
Unwinnable War

By 1971, the war had lasted for nine years and it had become clear to both sides, the Government and Anyanya High Command, that either way, it was un-winnable. Fortunately, some events and situations came up, which created the atmosphere and/or impetus for the two sides to reach a peace agreement. Those events included the following: Firstly, there was greater military pressure on the Government from the Anyanya in the wake of military assistance from Israel. Secondly, the fall of Milton Obote's Government in Uganda and his replacement by General Idi Amin, a Kakwa, and who was more sympathetic to the Southern rebel movement. As may be recalled, Obote was hostile to the Southern Resistance Movement; and at the behest of the Government of the Sudan, he allowed his troops to kill Fr Saturnino Ohure, on 22 January 1967. But under Amin, the Anyanya operatives could move much more freely in Uganda. Thirdly, there was the realization by both the Government of the Sudan and the Anyanya that they could not win in the battle field. Fourthly, the appointment of Abel Alier as the Minister for Southern Affairs, instead of Joseph Ukel Garang. Unlike many other previous Southern politicians who were part of the Northern-dominated governments in Khartoum, and who usually acquiesced to Northern designs against the Southerners, irrespective of how bad they were, acted differently. In contrast, he used his good relations with Nimeiri and his government to persuade them to go for a peaceful resolution of the Southern problem. For that reason, he contributed most of the ideas and stipulations in the Addis Ababa Agreement. Lastly, during this period, there too was a lot of pressure on Lagu by the international community, notably the World Council of Churches and the All-Africa Conference of Churches, to reach a peaceful settlement. All those reasons combined and pressurized the belligerents to talk peace.

PETER OBADAYO TINGWA

The Preliminary Talks and the Boost to the Talks (Sudan Airways Plane Crash)

Initial talks began in Addis Ababa in November 1971 between the Government of the Sudan, represented by Abel Alier, Minister for Southern Affairs and Mohamed El Baghir, Minister of Interior and the Anyanya South Sudan Liberation Movement (SSLM), represented by Frederick Magot Daŋgoro and Elisapana Käbi Mulla. A cessation of hostilities was agreed to for December 1971 and January 1972 and for the substantive negotiations to take place in February 1972.

While those preparations for the talks were going on, an incident occurred which gave great impetus for the talks. On 06 December 1971, a Sudan Airways aircraft crash landed at Dumule, in Lozo Payam, East Mundri County. The area was under the command of Major Repent Sunday. The expectation of the Government and the Northern population was that, all the Northerners in the aircraft would be killed by the Anyanya, if they survived the crash. That however did not happen, instead the Anyanya treated the survivors very well. They treated those who were injured and gave them food, water and dress. They then took them to the Sudan army garrison at Mundri. That story could not be believed by the Northerners who, until then, had been convinced by the Government that the Anyanya were killers and would kill Northerners at sight. Consequently, there was an atmosphere of goodwill and the Northerners put pressure on the Government to reach a settlement with the Anyanya. That gave impetus to the talks that had been started.

Ezboni Returns to Southern Politics
Head of the SSLM Delegation

As mentioned in earlier paragraphs, Ezboni had taken leave of Southern politics and he was teaching in Bombo Secondary School in Uganda and so was notably absent from the Southern Sudan, Nile, and Anyidi Provisional Governments and also was not part of the Anyanya Military Government. So, how much he knew about the impending peace agreement is not known. But after Frederick Magot and Elisapana Käbi Mulla returned with the schedule of substantial negotiations to end the conflict, there now arose a need for a more seasoned politician on the Anyanya side to take up the talks. For this, Lagu, needed to put forward a person with the stature, weight and experience in the politics of the Sudan as well as one who could stand tall in dealing with the machinations of the Northern Sudan. He initially considered Gordon Mourtat to head the delegation but when Gordon expressed misgivings about the talks, he quickly settled on Ezboni to head the talks. As was the case, Ezboni's name was well known to the Southerners as a staunch Southern nationalist. Additionally, Ezboni was well known to the Northern establishment and elites as a principled person, who could not be bribed. It is quite likely that Ezboni readily accepted Lagu's call and was appointed to lead the delegation of SSLM for the Addis Ababa talks and the members of the delegation were:

Mr. Ezboni Mondiri Gwonza	Head of Delegation
Dr. Lawrence Wol Wol	Secretary
Mr. Enock Mading de Garang	Spokesperson

Brig. Frederick Magot Daŋgoro   Military Representative
Mr. Oliver Batali Albino   Member
Mr. Angelo Voga Mursal   Member
Rev. Paul Pot   Member
Mr. Job Adier   Member

The Talks and the Agreement

The Talks began in February 1972. Since the proceedings of the Talks were not available to the writer, it is difficult to tell Ezboni's own contributions in it. The agreement, known as the Addis Ababa Agreement, was hammered out and duly signed on 03 March 1972. It was signed by Ezboni for the Southern Sudan Liberation Movement (Anyanya) and Abel Alier for the Government of the Sudan. What is clear, however, is that the Agreement contained many of the ingredients of Ezboni's Federal Manifesto of 1958. For example, the opening of the borders to East Africa so that some of the goods for Southern Sudan could come through that way. As a consequence, in the Agreement, the Regional Government was allowed to open a Purchasing Office in Nairobi.

Reaction to the Agreement

Reaction to the Agreement was very much varied. On the part of Southerners, those living inside the country generally accepted it, while those outside the country had divided opinions. Most of them, however, accepted it but some others criticized it on the grounds that it was far below what the people had shed blood for. Some of the leaders who did not accept the Agreement

Plate VII: Emperor Haile Selasie holds the hands of Ezboni Mondiri, Head of the SSLM Delegation and Abel Alier, Minister for Southern Affairs and Head of the Delegation of the Government of Sudan as they greet each other after the signing of the Addis Ababa Agreement on 27 February 1972

were persons like Gordon Mourtat and Aggrey Jaden. Joseph Oduho initially rejected it but later came around to accept it. Furthermore, some Southerners criticized it on the grounds that it was signed by two Southerners, Abel Alier and Ezboni Mondiri. To them, it should have been signed by a Northerner instead of Abel Alier, a Southerner. On the other hand, many Northerners felt that the Agreement was a sell-out to Southerners and that Nimeiri had given too much to them. Consequently, many of them denigrated it as Nimeiri's agreement with Southerners and so would have nothing to do with it. This stand on the part of some Northerners, as we shall see later, haunted the Agreement and eventually contributed to its downfall.

Ratification of the Agreement

After the signing of the Agreement, there was a strong pressure from the international community to have it ratified quickly. So, on 12 March 1972, SSLM/Anyanya ratified the Agreement, mostly on the grounds that a bird in hand is always better than the thousands flying out there. On the part of the Government, the Agreement was also ratied by the Assembly and was made to be an integral part of the organic law of the Sudan.

Implementation of the Agreement
The Southern Regional Government
(First contravention of the Agreement)

When the ink was dry, implementation of the Agreement began by the appointment of the President of the High Executive Council. President Gaafar Nimeiri appointed Abel Alier as the President of the High Executive Council (HEC) in contravention to the stipulations of the Agreement. Although Article 19 says that the President of HEC shall be appointed and relieved from office by the President of the Republic *"on the recommendation of the Peoples Regional Assembly"*. Ezboni, together with many other members of SSLM were not happy with Nimeiri's blatant violation of the Agreement in appointing Abel on his own. Ezboni led the protest about this and was quite vocal about it. He warned that if Nimeiri got away with that, nothing would

Plate VIII: The first Cabinet of the High Executive Council of the Southern Regional Government with President Nimeiri. Front row from left: Ezboni Mondiri, Toby Maduot, Vice President El Baghir, President Nimeiri, Abel Alier, Hilary Logali and Joseph Oduho. Back row from left: Lawrence Wol Wol, Michael Tawil, Gama Hassan, Enock Mading de Garang, Natale Olwak.

prevent him from doing the same in future in respect to other stipulations of the Agreement. How prophetic he was! As will be seen later, President Nimeiri violated the Agreement several times, including abrogating it completely. Thereafter, a Cabinet was appointed with eleven members. Ezboni was was one of the members of the Cabinet as the Minister of Communications and Transport.

As for the Major General Joseph Lagu, Chief of the Anyanya High Command and Chairman of the Southern Sudan Liberation Movement (SSLM), President Nimeiri promoted him to the rank of a General in the Sudan Army and assigned him to be in charge of the Sudan Army First Division in Southern Sudan, which is headquartered in Juba. The Anyanya forces were integrated into the Sudan Army as per the Agreement and the repatriation of refugees began.

CHAPTER XIV: IN THE SOUTHERN SUDAN REGIONAL GOVERNMENT (SSRG)

This period is a very critical one in the political and socio-economic evolution and development of the people of Southern Sudan since foreign intervention began in the middle of 1800s. It marked the first time they ever were to be in charge of some of their own affairs, though not all. It also marked the period when the Southerners related directly with one another politically, economically, socially and ethnically without the Northerners. Hilary Logali in his memoirs dubbed it "Our Kingdom Come?" which he denoted with a question mark and underscored it with what he called "fissiparous tendencies". For Ezboni, although it was less than the federation he desired, in conversations with the writer, he viewed it as fitting into his long-held vision of a critical stepping stone that would lead to the ultimate goal of independence of Southern Sudan. To him, it still offered some good opportunity for the Southerners to build their capacity for that final effort and push for independence.

Ezboni as the Minister of Communication and Transport in SSRG
Achievements

Ezboni embarked on his assignment with gusto. The first major task that fell on his lap was the urgent need to tarmac the main Juba roads in time for the celebration of the first anniversary of signing the Agreement due on 03 March 1973. That occasion was to be graced by Emperor Haile Selassie of Ethiopia, a key facilitator of the Peace Agreement. The task represented the first time ever that a road or street was being tarmacked in Juba. It was such that Ezboni and his senior executives Joseph Tambura, Serafino Wani and others were always at the site of the work; and for that reason, the tarmacking was completed in record time before the celebrations. This is in contrast to the tarmacking of the same length of the roads, after the Comprehensive Peace Agreement (CPA), where with a lot more money and even better equipment, it took two years or more for it to be completed. Another major development under his watch was the beginning of the construction of the Juba Bridge which replaced the ferry and which greatly improved the link with the East African countries.

Additionally, under his watch, many other bridges were reconstructed. For example, the Mundri Bridge across River Yei by British Army Engineers. Furthermore several agreements were reached under his watch to repair the main trunk roads that tied Equatoria to Bahr El Ghazal, the Juba- Mundri-Rumbek–Wau; and the Mundri-Yambio- Wau Roads, though some stretches were completed by subsequent Ministers.

Plate IX: HEC President Abel Alier cutting the ribbon to open the Juba Bridge. Looking on to his right is Dr. Beshir Abbadi, National Minister of Roads and Transport; and to his left are Ezboni Mondiri and Serafino Swaka

Differences with Abel, President of HEC

While those were going on, soon differences emerged between Ezboni and Abel Alier. One of those reasons emanated from the fact that Ezboni considered Abel as a person who has been imposed by Nimeiri to do his (Nimeiri's) bidding or fulfill Northern designs in the post-Addis Ababa Agreement era. The second one was that, as it happened, the absorption of the Anyanya into the Sudan Army was not transparently carried out, since many non-Anyanya individuals succeeded to be absorbed into the Army; and as a consequence, many genuine and deserving Anyanya soldiers were left out, As a result many of those left out became angry and rebellious and Ezboni sympathized with them. Hence, Abel suspected Ezboni to be behind that rebelliousness. Ezboni was therefore suspected to be having some arms stowed away somewhere and because of that, security personnel and police mowed down Ezboni's sweet potato mounds on the suspicious that he could be hiding weapons there.

The First Elections After the Addis Ababa Agreement
Gerrymandering

As per the Agreement, elections were to be held in 1973. However, instead of using the old constituencies, at the behest of President Nimeiri and Abel Alier, the Election Commission made some arbitrary constituencies in which the Moru Constituency was amalgamated with the Pojulu areas of Lainya and Yondoru as one constituency. The reason behind that gerrymandering was to ensure that Ezboni does not come to the Regional Assembly to cause problems. Moreover, when the time of polling came, many of the voters in Moru land did not find their names because their names had been sent to different polling stations. Ezboni and the Moru people were sure that the amalgamation of Constituency as well as the sending of lists to wrong polling stations were deliberately done by Abel in connivance with Nimeiri to deny Ezboni entrance into the Regional Assembly. So, inevitably, when the elections were done, Ezboni lost and Eliaba James Surur won that constituency. After the election, a new cabinet was formed but Ezboni was still retained as the Minister for Communication and Transport, perhaps, as a way to placate him.

Transfer to the North

Ezboni lost his ministerial appointment in one of the reshuffles. Instead of leaving him idle in the South, Abel agreed with Nimeiri to appoint him as the Managing Director of the proposed Melut Sugar Scheme. That meant that he had to go and live in Khartoum. Ezboni, however, strongly believed that the assignment was a way devised by Abel and Nimeiri to get rid of him from Southern Sudan. Moreover at this point, Abel's relationship with both Clement Mboro and Joseph Oduho had ebbed and he did not like Ezboni to be around or to join that opposition. Ezboni took up the assignment and went to live in Khartoum. But soon he found out that the Northerners were really not keen to start the sugar schemes that were proposed to be established in Southern Sudan, that were Melut and Mongalla Sugar Schemes. They therefore were not keen to start the schemes and deprived both the proposed Sugar Schemes of funds. That was in sharp contrast to the proposed sugar schemes in Northern Sudan, like Northwest Sennar and Haggar Asalaya, which were plentifully funded. Since the Melut Sugar was not functioning, Ezboni had nothing to do. So, he became frustrated and became more convinced that, in his own words, he had deliberately been shunted from the politics of Southern Sudan by Abel and Nimeiri.

Politics in Southern Region

While Ezboni was in Khartoum, politics in Southern Region had become polarized into two camps: Abel's Group and Lagu's Group. Abel's Group was mostly constituted of the members of the defunct Southern Front Party and who dominated the Government. Its leadership comprised of Southern Front stalwarts like Hilary Logali, Henry Bago, Lubari Ramba, Luigi Adwok, Isaiah Kulang, and others. The Group was generally supported by those Southerners who remained in the country. The other Group, which actually was in opposition, was led by General Joseph Lagu. It comprised of the leadership of the SSLM, Ezboni Mondiri, Joseph Oduho, Lawrence Wol Wol and others. This Group generally allied itself with the SANU of William Deng, led by Samuel Aru, Toby Maduot, Ezekiel Kodi, Andrew Wiew and others. Clement Mboro occupied a position in between the two, though towards the end he was leaning more to the SANU/SSLM Group. Also, during this period, there was a growing disenchantment with Abel's Government, over several issues, one of which was the digging of the Jonglei Canal, where many Southerners believed Abel had acquiesced to Northern demands and sold the South.

The Elections of 1978 and Lagu's Change 2 Government

Advisor to Lagu

When the elections of 1978 came round, Ezboni resigned from being the General Manager of Melut Sugar Factory and went for the elections. With Mundri Constituency restored, Ezboni won handily, and Lagu's Group, calling itself 'Change 2', won the overall elections. Many of Abel's prominent ministers like Hilary Logali, Gama Hassan and others lost in the elections. With the majority of seats in the Assembly in his camp, Lagu became the President of HEC with Samuel Aru Bol as Deputy to Lagu, while Ezboni became an Advisor to the President. In view of that, Abel then left for Khartoum to perform his duties as the Second Vice President of the country.

Upon assumption of the office, many people were happy with the changes that Lagu made, particularly the removal of Reuben Mac, the Chief of the Police in Southern Sudan. Most people of Equatoria, especially in Juba, did not like Reuben Mac because they saw him as an arch tribalist. He was seen to be favoring his Dinka tribesmen, especially from Bor. That was clear in his recruitment of police into the service as well as in only sending Dinka candidates to the Police College in Khartoum. But soon Lagu's Government began to face problems. The flow of money from Khartoum became irregular and consequently, salaries were often delayed. Also, the flow of grains from the North slowed down; and as a result, there were pockets of famine in several parts of Southern Sudan. Lagu felt that all those problems were caused by Abel in revenge for his loss of the elections.

But though Abel could have been played a role in making things difficult to Lagu, Lagu himself made some errors and which Abel's Group seized on to criticize him. According to Ezboni, he used to advise Lagu as to either a course of action to take or as to how to respond to issues. He told the writer of two cases, where Lagu wasn't happy with his advice. One was about his advice to Lagu not to receive some of Amin's Generals, who had taken refuge in Juba, in the HEC Presidential office, lest the new government in Uganda construe that as Sudan's support for the rebels. He advised that if Lagu really wanted to see them, they could see him privately in his home. Lagu did not like that advice. Secondly, he told the writer that on one occasion, when Lagu went to the Customs Office in connection with clearance of some goods and later his name was later embroiled in the clearance scandal of those goods, he reminded him that his (Lagu's) going to the Customs Office was incompatible with the office he was holding; and that if that were in advanced countries, he Lagu would have to resign. That advice did not sit well with Lagu and he promptly dismissed Ezboni.

Interestingly on that very day of his dismissal, the writer was in Ezboni's government residence. At around 2:30 pm, Ezboni burst into the house from the office and ordered the family to pack all family belongings for immediate move to his private home in the *malakia*. All were perplexed! In response, he told the writer that Lagu had relieved him of the post and that he did not want to grant Lagu the pleasure of kicking him out of the government house. In about two hours, a truck arrived and carried the family to his house in the *malakia*. Ezboni remained in the house and at around 5:30 pm an official arrived from the HEC and handed him Lagu's letter about his dismissal. He received the letter and handed the house and the official vehicle assigned to him and left for his home in the *malakia*.

However, after Ezboni's departure, Lagu's Government ran into more problems and was facing criticism from many corners. His Deputy Samuel Aru was in a problem for depositing some government money in his own private account. Hence, Lagu became so desperate to the extent that in order to shore up the image of his government, he even went as far as to bring some of Abel's people into his government, such as Natale Olwak, Martin Majier, Ambrose Ring, Peter Gatkuoth and others. In view of all those, and allegedly with Abel's connivance, Nimeiri dissolved Lagu's Government in 1980 and appointed Peter Gatkuoth as an Interim President of HEC, pending and election in 1982.

CHAPTER XV: THE LOOMING THREAT TO THE SSRG AND THE ADISS ABABA AGREEMENT

The Election of 1982 and Abel's Second Government

Harbinger of Events

When the elections were held, Ezboni won again in the Mundri Constituency. But the overall elections were won by Abel's Group, and so Abel came back to be the President of HEC. According to Hilary in his memoirs, in his effort to win the Presidency again, Abel, consciously or not, relied very heavily on pan-Dinka support. In that, he was even supported by those Dinkas who were not from Bor or in Southern Front. That shift on the part of Abel to his tribesmen scuttled Hilary Logali's aspirations for the presidency of the HEC.

During Abel's second term, Ezboni was still not on good terms with Abel, though he was not part of the group that was opposing Abel and his regime. It was, however, during this second period of Abel that many of the events happened regionally and nationally that led to the abrogation of the Addis Ababa Agreement and ultimately to the re- division of Southern Sudan (*kokora*). As a staunch Southern nationalist, *kokora* came as a shock to Ezboni. It shattered his dream of ultimate independence of Southern Sudan which hinged on the unity of the Southern Sudanese. In his words to the writer, it represented one of the saddest episodes in the political history of the people of Southern Sudan. Though Ezboni had nothing to do with why and how *kokora* came about, it may be appropriate to briefly outline the events and factors that caused it for an appreciation of the whole story.

Endogenous Regional Factors and Causes

Several events and factors occurred in the Southern Regional Government that provoked the demand for the re-division of Southern Sudan by some Southerners, especially among the people of Equatoria and those include:

Joseph Lagu left the seat of the HEC a bitter man. He was sure that it was Abel who was responsible for his removal and he was thus determined to revenge;

The rallying of all the Dinka behind Abel's candidacy for the presidency of HEC. Those actions, coupled with careless statements from a few Dinkas of 'born to rule' and '*Alier tok*' and exacerbated by tribal fights in the schools, created a growing resentment of the Dinkas by many people of Equatoria;

Abel's prompt return of Reuben Mac as Chief of Police in

Southern Region, to the chagrin of the people of Juba and of Equatoria, after he had been removed by Joseph Lagu (NB: most people of Equatoria saw Reuben as an arch tribalist)

Abel's appointments smacked of overt tribalism and nepotism. For example, he appointed Yithak Wel, an intermediate school leaver from his area, as Director General of Education, over and above several senior teachers who were graduates of universities like Joseph Kabulu, Anderea Modi and many others. Furthermore, Abel appointed Zakaria Ngor, a very junior executive in the Ministry of Finance and Economic Planning as the Managing Director of the Mongalla Agro-industrial Project over and above more senior executives in the Ministries of Agriculture and Economic Planning. In addition to the above, at that time, several Dinka Bor cattle herders had moved and established cattle camps in Mundari and Bari areas around Mongalla and Juba town. Their presence had created friction and resentment among the Bari towards the Dinka.

All these combined to engender an anti-Dinka and anti-Abel feelings among the people of Equatoria.

Exogenous National Factors and Causes

Nationally, there were events and factors that combined with the regional factors to bring about *kokora*. They include:

Generally, the Northerners were really not very enthusiastic about the Addis Ababa Agreement dubbing it a sell out to the Southerners. So, they could care less if it were to go;

Implementation of regionalism in the North, where the provinces was elevated to Regions. Some people of Equatoria liked the idea as a way to get rid of Dinkas;

President Nimeiri's acceptance of the recommendations of the 1977 National Reconciliation Conference held in Port Sudan by Northern political parties. That reconciliation was done without the participation of Southerners. In that conference, Nimeiri accepted and committed himself to reducing what the Northern political parties considered as excessive powers given to the Southern Regional Government. He thus began to seek ways of how to reduce those powers;

The discovery of oil in Bentiu area in Southern Sudan in 1978. That discovery injected a huge and new dimension into the politics of the Sudan, especially the North-South dichotomy. The Northerners suddenly woke up to the fact that, henceforth, the economy of the Sudan would be relying on Southern Sudan, a region which they and the British had consistently despised as economically worthless. They therefore resorted to confuse the location of the oil fields by consistently describing it to fall in an area 400 kilometers south west of Khartoum;

The rejection by the Abel and the SSRG of the attempts to annex the oil fields to be part of the North through: a) creating Bentiu area, to be a province and to be called Unity Province; and that Province to be directly under the President. In other words, the area would be part of the North; and b) tampering with the 1956 border by moving it southwards so as to include the oil fields in Panthou in the North. Abel and the SSRG's rejection was based on the facts that the Addis Ababa Agreement, which was now part of the Constitution, would not allow it;

The disagreement between President Nimeiri' and Abel Alier (Southern Regional Government), regarding the location of the refinery for local consumption. Nimeiri and the Northerners wanted it to be located in Kosti, while Abel and the Southern

Regional Government wanted it to be located in Bentiu; and Lastly, whereas President Nimeiri used to be welcomed enthusiastically in the South, in his last visit to Rumbek and Bor, he was greeted with demonstrations. He thus considered Abel to be responsible for the hostile reception he received

Thus President Nimeiri felt that the Addis Ababa Agreement and the Southern Regional Government had become an obstacle to his and the North's plans and so must be removed or cut down to size.

Enter Hassan El Turabi with Sharia Agenda

One of the major exogenous factors that ensured the implementation of *kokora* was the entrance of Hassan El Turabi into the Government with his agendum of Sharia. That was, after the Charter of National Reconciliation between the Northern political parties in 1977, the leader of the Islamic Charter Front, Hassan El Turabi came into the Government. Soon, Hassan El Turabi succeeded to mesmerize and make Nimeiri an Islamic fundamentalist with a view of bringing Sharia laws to the Sudan. El Turabi however knew that, if the Addis Ababa Agreement and the Southern Regional Government were there, Sharia law would never be implemented in the Sudan. Because, Articles 14 and 15 of the Addis Ababa Agreement, which permit the Southern Regional Assembly (SRA) to petition the President to remove any national laws which have been passed by the National Assembly and which the SRA considers to be inimical to Southern Sudan. So, El Turabi knew that with those stipulations in place, Sharia would never be implemented in the Sudan, since the Southern Regional Government would petition the President to remove it. He therefore began to seek ways of how to remove the Addis Ababa Agreement and the Southern Regional Government from the scene.

Plot Against the Addis Ababa Agreement
Proposing Re-Division (Kokora)

As narrated in earlier paragraphs, and after being relieved from the presidency of HEC, Lagu went to Khartoum, a very bitter man who felt that Abel was responsible for the demise of his Government. So, he began to seek ways of how to revenge on Abel. For this, he seized on the growing anti-Abel and especially the anti-Dinka feeling in Equatoria and produced a booklet showing how the Dinka were dominating the Southern Regional Government. Consequently, he suggested that the Southern Region should be re-divided into three Regions (Bahr El Ghazal, Equatoria and Upper Nile) so as to be like the Regions in the North. Whether he was cognizant of the fact that such an action would not only remove Abel from HEC, but would automatically abrogate the Addis Ababa Agreement, is difficult to tell now. Ezboni and many Southerners were shocked about this proposal and wondered as to how Lagu, of all people, could come up with such an idea? An idea which would not only remove the Addis Ababa Agreement for which many people died but also weaken the Southerners in respect to Northern machinations. Nonetheless, a lot of the younger leadership of Equatoria and a good percentage of the general people of Equatoria came to support Lagu's proposal. Their main reasons for embracing that proposal emanated from the endogenous factors and events that had been listed in an earlier paragraph.

The Triple Plotters: Nimeiri, Lagu and El Turabi

The plotters against the Addis Ababa Agreement and the SSRG were President Nimeiri, Hassan El Turabi and Joseph Lagu. A situation had arisen in which the three persons found a common cause to bring down Abel's Government and consequently the Addis Ababa Agreement; and each for his own reason. For Nimeiri, it was so that the Regional Government would not stand in his way, regarding national issues; as well as to fulfill his commitment to the Northern political parties in the National Reconciliation Charter in Port Sudan in 1977 to reduce the powers of the Southern Regional Government. For El Turabi, it was for paving the way for the implementation of the Sharia. For Lagu, it was for avenging what he felt had been done to him by Abel and for getting rid of Dinka domination, especially from Equatoria. So, to Nimeiri, El Turabi and the Northerners in general, Lagu's proposal was a God-send manna from heaven which they had been looking for. The trio therefore began to look for ways of bringing it about.

Letting the Cat out of the Bag

After the trio, had worked on it behind the scenes and felt that they had mobilized sufcient support for it, they considered that it was time to bring the issue out in the open as a policy of the SSU party. The occasion and venue they chose was the ruling party's National Congress in March 1981 in Khartoum. In his opening address, the Chairman President Nimeiri shocked many members of Southern delegation that he had received a petition from some Southerners, requesting the tabling of the issue of the re-division of the Southern Region before the National Congress. In reaction, those Southern attendants, who opposed the idea of re-division, protested and reminded the President that, that would be un-procedural, since the issue had not been discussed at the Regional level, as required by the SSU rules and regulations. Additionally, they reminded the President that, that would also contravene the stipulations of the Addis Ababa Agreement, since the Southern Regional Assembly had not discussed it. In view of those arguments, President Nimeiri withdrew the topic of re-division from the agenda, but directed that the Southern delegation to go back to Juba, discuss the matter and send him the recommendations.

Anger and Disagreement over the Proposal

When the Southern delegation returned to Juba, Abel and his group were angry with the proponents and were determined to stamp out the idea of re-division, because they saw it as a Northern plot to weaken the Southern Sudanese through divide and rule and resume their domination of the Southerners once again. He therefore called the SSU Assembly Body, under the chairmanship of Ambrose Ring. The aim of Abel and his group was for that meeting to come up with the rejection of re-division and consequently inform Nimeiri accordingly.

Ezboni was in that meeting and according to him, the discussions were conducted in the most undemocratic way. Those who wanted the meeting to find out as to whether there were any justifiable reasons as to why some Southerners were asking for re-division were either shouted down or were not given the chance to speak. Only those who condemned *kokora* in extreme language were allowed to speak. Ezboni told the writer that he wanted to say that there indeed were some issues which had caused that feeling and that they must not be pushed under the carpet. But he was not given the chance. Given that, and particularly the manner in which Ambrose Ring was conducting the meeting, he was disappointed to the extent that he walked out of the meeting before the resolution.

The meeting ended up by rejecting the re-division of the Southern Region and recommended that President Nimeiri should be informed accordingly. Ezboni's walk out was misunderstood by both opponents and proponents of re- division. So many from both sides saw it as an indication of his support for re-division of the South, whereas it was not. Thereafter, the outcome was communicated to President Nimeiri that re- division had been rejected by the Southern Regional SSU Assembly Body; and subsequently, based on that, Abel warned that anybody who would talk again about re-division would be promptly arrested.

The threat by Abel forced the supporters of re-division to go underground. Now under a secret organization, Equatoria Central Committee, and calling the re-division, *kokora* in Bari language, they established direct links with Nimeiri, Lagu and El Turabi in Khartoum. In the meantime, tension began to rise between the Dinka and the people of Equatoria and the politicians became divided into two groups: Unionists under Abel and comprising of persons like Isaiah Kulang, Bona Malwal, Joseph Oduho, Hilary Logali, Lubari Ramba, and many others; and Re-divisionists under Joseph Lagu. Those included persons like Dhol Acuil, Mathew Obur, Daniel Kuot Mathews from the other provinces and Francis Wajo, Joseph James Tambura, Pacifico

Lolik, Luka Monoja, Eliaba James Surur, Philip Yona and many others from Equatoria. Ezboni however kept his views about the pros and cons of re- division to himself. He first wanted to obtain clarifications from Nimeiri and Lagu on serious matters which re-division could raise, like the fate of the Addis Ababa Agreement. He therefore decided to go to Khartoum to meet Nimeiri and Lagu.

Seeking Clarifications from President Nimeiri and Joseph Lagu

In Khartoum, Ezboni sought audience with President Nimeiri. But possibly anticipating what Ezboni was going to say, he declined to meet him. Instead, the President sent a message to Ezboni saying that he should see First Vice President El Baghir, who was with him in the Addis Ababa talks. Ezboni declined that offer. He wanted to talk to Nimeiri on this and no other. He therefore went to Lagu for a one-on- one meeting. According to him, he asked Lagu as to what and how the fate of the Addis Ababa would be under a re-divided Southern Sudan. He also enquired as to how the Southerners could come together in the event that the Northerners went back to do sinister things to the Southerners. According to him, Lagu did not give him very satisfactory answers to those two questions. So, he came to the conclusion that Lagu did not have a plan B for *kokora* if it went sour, and so it was not good for the people of Southern Sudan. He also wondered as to how Lagu, of all people, could be so callous about the Agreement for which the people of Southern Sudan sacrificed dearly with their blood. That also confimed his conviction that President Nimeiri and the

Northerners were using Lagu and the issue of re- division for abrogating the Addis Ababa Agreement, so as to bring the South back under their domination. As a person who believed strongly in Southerners working themselves out of unitary Sudan through regionalism or federalism, he concluded that *kokora* was not good for Southerners and decided to fight it.

Ezboni Reconciles with Abel and Becomes a Unionist

Ezboni came back to Juba and the very next day he went to Abel in the HEC. He told Abel that for the sake of Southern Sudan, they should bury their differences, since the South was about to be destroyed. Abel wholeheartedly expressed his happiness and consent with Ezboni's view and both worked out a strategy in which Ezboni would use his popular standing amongst the Southern Sudanese to go around Southern Sudan to warn the people about the danger of *kokora*. Consequently, Abel gave Ezboni a vehicle and sufficient fuel for going around. Ezboni toured as much areas in Bahr El Ghazal, Upper Nile and Equatoria, warning the people that *kokora* was an agenda of the Northerners to divide them and then take away the little freedom they fought and died for and which had been encapsulated in the Addis Ababa Agreement and enshrined in the Constitution. His words were well received in many places, especially in Bahr El Ghazal and Upper Nile.

Nimeiri Dissolves the Abel's Second Government

By the time Ezboni completed the tour, Nimeiri had dissolved both the National and Regional Assemblies and called for new elections at the end of one year. In the South, he appointed Retired General Gismalla Abdalla Rassas, Plate 1 (x), to head the HEC in the interim period. The Unionists were distrustful of him but the Re-divisionists accepted him. Rassas took the seat but when he was in it, he began to do things that tended to support the Unionist point of view. He made efforts to cool down the tempers between the opponents and supporters of *kokora*. He even began some decentralization of posts in the Southern Region. For example, he raised the position of the senior inspector of education at Wau Juba and Malakal to the level of a Director. But this did not sit well with the *kokora* people. To them it was like Rassas was going to obfuscate the issue of *kokora*, and they communicated this to Nimeiri. So, when Rassas' cabinet asked for an extension of their period, Nimeiri refused. It is possible that had Rassas been given an extension or stayed longer, perhaps *kokora* might not have happened.

The Elections of April 1983, Joseph Tambura as President of HEC

The dominant issue and the campaign in the elections was *kokora* between the Unionists and the Re-divisionists. Ezboni, who was vehemently opposed to *kokora* stood in his usual Constituency of Mundri as a Unionist. On the other hand, Brown Elemetu, a local merchant, stood as the candidate for *kokora* (Re-divisionists). Ezboni campaigned very hard, reminding the people that behind the re-division the Northerners were lurking ready to take away the gains that the Addis Ababa Agreement had brought. He was assisted in his campaigns against re-division by Benjamin Warille, Natania Baya and Paul Tier. But with the wave of anti-Dinka feeling raging in Equatoria, and even in Moru land, his opponents mounted an effective campaign against him. He was projected as one who had accepted Dinka domination. Hence, for the very first time, barring his loss to Eliaba Surur when the Mundri/Amadi Constituency was merged with the Pojulu constituency, he lost the election to Brown Elemetu.

At the Regional level, the results were such that supporters of Re- division won the majority of seats and so they chose Joseph James Tambura, Plate 1(l), to be the President of the HEC. With the Re- divisionists in power, there was nothing for him to do. But he would tell anybody who came to him that the idea of re-division was a blunder by the people of Southern Sudan.

Kokora Decreed, Addis Ababa Agreement Abrogated

When Tambura was firmly in power, he connived with Nimeiri to effect the *kokora* by decree, though both knew it was against the stipulations of the Addis Ababa Agreement. As told, Nimeiri instructed him to put that down as a request to him (as President of the country) as the head of the Southern Regional Government to dissolve the Southern Regional Government and from it, create three new Regional Governments in Malakal, Juba and Wau. Accordingly, Tambura wrote the letter. Thus on 05 June 1983, President Nimeiri decreed the dissolution of the Southern Regional government, together with the establishment three weaker Regional Governments in Juba, Malakal and Wau of similar powers to the Regions in the North. So, James

Tambura, Daniel Kuot Mathews and Lawrence Wol Wol were respectively appointed to be Governors in the new Regions. By this, the Addis Ababa Agreement was indirectly and effectively abrogated.

So, while the Re-divisionists celebrated, the Unionists mourned the fate of Southern Sudan. When the writer expressed his sadness at the dissolution of the Southern Regional Government to Ezboni, he replied that it was good that *kokora* had been effected. Because, he said, "if it had not been done, our people would have continued to feel that something good had been denied to them"; adding that they would, however, "sooner or later find out that it was not as good as they had thought".

Therefore, with *kokora* in place, the Northerners achieved the goal they had agreed to in 1977 in the National Reconciliation Charter in Port Sudan to reduce the powers given to the Southerners. A sad episode of the *kokora* was that, although it was a national project, the national government did not give enough funds for implementing it. Instead, it asked for the assets of the now defunct Southern Regional Government to be divided amongst the three new Regions. This became a source of serious quarrels between the Regions, especially since some of the assets were indivisible. It was thus very pathetic to see very senior government officials quarreling over such mundane things as tables, tea sets, table fans and so on.

The Decreeing of the Sharia Laws and Reactions

With the Addis Ababa Agreement and Southern Regional Government out of the way, it was now easy for El Turabi and Nimeiri to bring about the Sharia laws. So, in September

1983, President Nimeiri decreed the Sharia laws to be the legal system for the whole of Sudan. Many Southerners, including the proponents of *kokora* were shocked by it. In Juba, following the decree, the town's people gathered in the Malakia Football Club to march to the now Equatoria Regional Executive Council to hand a letter of protest against the Sharia laws. Ironically, this was the same venue and same crowd that used to march and make demands for *kokora*. As the throng of demonstrators passed by the University of Juba on its way to the Regional Executive Council, chanting anti-Sharia slogans and singing *"We will never, never surrender"*, Hilary Logali, who at that moment happened to be watching the crowd with the writer commented that "Our people have chosen to learn the hard way. Because, when we were warning them that the weakening of the South through *kokora* would bring such bad eventualities, they did not believe us".

Ezboni Appointed General Manager of Nzara Industrial Complex

In the new Equatoria Region, Joseph James Tambura was the Governor and Francis Wajo was Deputy Governor. At about the beginning of 1984, they persuaded Khartoum to appoint Ezboni as the Managing Director of the Nzara Agricultural Industrial Complex. Ezboni himself thought that the appointment was to get him out of Juba. Anyway, he went to Nzara to assume the post but there he was met with hostility from some of the younger Zande intellectuals headed by Louis Tanda. They felt that the post should have been given to a Zande, probably to one of them. After a couple of days in Nzara, Ezboni returned to

Juba and was shocked to find copy of a letter to him. The letter, which the writer had a chance to read was written to Governor Tambura, with a copies to Nimeiri and to Ezboni and the letter was signed by Louis Tanda and other Zande intellectuals. The letter said that Ezboni, had no degree, was old, incompetent and so did not qualify for that post; and that post should have gone to such very qualified and younger individuals like Louis Tanda. Ezboni felt very much insulted and he told the writer that, since his school days and through his working and political life, that was the first time ever for him to be called unqualified and incompetent. He felt hurt because he did not ask to be considered for that post; and more so, because the insults were by persons whom he considered to be his children. He therefore decided not to take up the post and even not to return to Nzara again.

CHAPTER XVI:
THE CLOSING YEARS

A New Resistance Movement, the Sudan Peoples' Liberation Movement (SPLM)

As all the above were going on in the Sudan, in May 1983, a new Southern Resistance Movement began in Bor, Jonglei Province, headed by Col. John Garang de Mabior. The focus of the new movement was on the liberation of the whole Sudan and not of Southern Sudan. How much Ezboni knew or cared to know about the objectives or aims of the new movement is hard to tell today. But as diehard Southern nationalist, he must have wondered, like many others, how the liberation of the Sudan was going to get Southern Sudan on the way to independence.

War and Military Takeover
Exile in Khartoum

From Bor, the SPLM War spread to many parts of Greater Upper Nile. In the mid to end of 1980s, it had reached Equatoria. In 1989, a group of Islamic fundamentalist army officers, led by Omar Ahmed El Bashir, overthrew the civilian government of PM Saddig El Mahdi and they established a National Salvation Government. The new government just took over when it was four days before a peace talks between PM Saddig El Mahdi's Government and the SPLM/A could take place. It was an Islamic fundamentalist government.

For a while, Ezboni stayed in Juba doing nothing. But as the war intensified, like everybody else, he moved to Khartoum in the early 1990s. He at first resided in Abbasia in Omdurman. But as his financial situation got worse, he moved to Karton Kassala, an unplanned abode of the poor and the marginalized, at the out skirts of Hag Yousif Residential Area. The area was named so because, all the residences were made of cartons and sacks. He enjoyed his stay among the poor and they in turn appreciated his coming down to live with them. His financial situation was very bad, since he did not steal public money nor got bribed like many other politicians. He also could not bring himself down to go and ask for assistance from either the government of El Beshir or from the Equatoria Regional Government.

At the beginning of the 1990s the regime began to toy with the idea of federation in the country. They appointed Ezboni to be one of the members of a High Committee for Implementation of the Federal System in the country, Ezboni was unenthusiastic about it simply because he knew the federal system which the government had in mind differed substantially from his own. Just by being in that Committee, Ezboni could have easily obtained money from El Beshir's Islamic fundamentalist government, since that government was by then desperately looking for very senior Southern politicians to join them, to give respectability to their government in the eyes of Southern Sudanese or the world at large. But Ezboni could and would not do that. To him, that would have been tantamount to prostituting himself to Northerners, especially of the worst kind, the Islamic fundamentalists.

It is worth pointing out here that Ezboni's strong disinclination to ask for assistance must also have arisen from the Moru culture which abhors begging. In Moru language, the word '*ele*' could mean 'begging', but it also carries a very shameful and derogatory content. One could be embarrassed or put down by the mere mention that he/she or member of his/her family '*ka ele*' (is begging) for whatever. This is probably why the Moru in urban areas are very rarely seen as beggars.

The End: Sickness and Ezboni Passes On

Ezboni considered his living in Khartoum as living in foreign exile. By 1991, with no income and consequent poor living conditions, his health began to decline. He used to ride the common Hag Yousif buses to town and occasionally could be seen walking from the town center to the Equatoria Coordination Office in El Amarat. In August, he suffered a stroke with concomitant attack of low blood sugar. By the time he was rushed to the hospital, he was already in coma. He needed an urgent infusion of very concentrated glucose (50%) to raise his blood sugar but the hospital did not have that concentration at hand. The writer with Dr. James Odrande moved to many pharmacies in the Three Towns but could not find any. They could only find the moderate concentrations (25%). Desperate efforts were undertaken by the doctors to raise his blood sugar, using the 25% but they were not successful. So, on Friday 27 September 1991 Ezboni passed away in Khartoum Civil Hospital at about midday. His remains were taken to Juba for burial.

In Khartoum, on Friday 02 October, the Government Newspaper, *The New Horizon* carried a news item titled *"The Father of Federal System is Dead!"* In the newspaper, El Beshir, the President of the Revolutionary Command Council eulogized him; and among other things, he described Ezboni as a strong advocate of peace and pioneer in the laying down the foundation of national political work. His Deputy Al Zubair Mohamed Salih also paid tribute to Ezboni. Full text of the news article is given in Appendix II.

The same issue of *The New Horizon* carried the editorial titled *"One of Federalism's Torches Goes out"* and lamented Ezboni's death. The editorial described him as pioneer advocate for federal system in the country and that he had called for federation at a time, when calling for federation was considered treason; and for that reason, he was sent to jail. The editorial described Ezboni as a person who was "filled with love for his people, country and freedom" and that he was a person who did not give up and also who had "confidence in himself that one day what he was championing (federation) for Sudan would come true". The editorial went on to say that in the Addis Ababa negotiations, Ezboni's view for federalism was considered too radical and was discarded for a weaker term, regionalism; and that when he was a Minister (in the Transitional Government of Sir El Khatim), the anti- federalist forces made sure he was out of the post.

The editorial pointed out that Ezboni did not like *kokora* and goes on to say that now with the Revolutionary Salvation Government poised to implement federalism, Ezboni must have been happy that his dream was about to come true. The editorial concluded by stating that Ezboni had done his work well and that, although federalism had not yet been realized, "the idea he advocated will never be forgotten. He has gone down in the history of the Sudan as a patriot who lit the way for the people to follow"

A memorial service was held in Khartoum in his honor and it was attended by Hilary Logali, Abel Alier and other Southern politicians. It was also attended by senior Government officials and a representative of the Commissioner of Khartoum Region. In the eulogy given by Hilary Logali, he described Ezboni one of the earliest Southern nationalists and father of federalism. He described it ironic that federalism for which Ezboni spent six years in jail was being considered as a solution for the problems of the Sudan.

As mentioned previously, Ezboni's remains were flown to Juba and were buried in Nyakuron cemetery. But in 2010, they were exhumed from Juba and were taken to Mundri for reburial, befittingly in front of the County Headquarters.

CHAPTER XVII:
EZBONI, THE MAN, POLITICIAN AND NATIONALIST

Introduction

In reading through the book one will certainly come up with their own views and conclusions as to the personality, character, views, convictions, courage, performance challenges, struggles, humiliations, sacrifices of which defined Ezboni during his struggle for federation for Southern Sudan, as a stepping stone, and ultimately for the freedom and independence of Southern Sudan. In this last Chapter, are two views about Ezboni the man: my views (writer); and that of Dr. David Bassiouni. Those views are presented below.

The Writer's Views

Several adjectives could be used to describe Ezboni. He was a taciturn who did not say much and rarely participates in ordinary banter, except with a few close friends. He also was not an orator to persuade people with eloquent and lofty speeches. His messages were always short to the point and once he had made the point he would always leave the audience hanging to complete the story or to reach their own conclusions. Ezboni would not over stay his welcome and would leave as soon as an event was over. This kind of behavior usually left an air of mystery about him, with the people wanting to know more about him or what he really was. His successes in elections many times over could in part be traced to this behavior.

Ezboni usually made quick decisions and once he has made the decision, he rarely would reverse it. His relatives knew this very well about him. For example, if Ezboni visits and they desire to serve him tea, soft drinks or food, they do it as quickly as they can. That is because Ezboni could suddenly get up to leave. And once he gets up to leave, no amount of pleading can convince him to sit down again to partake of what was being offered. It is reported that this impulsive behavior saved him from his pursuers after the fall of Lomileŋwa. Reportedly, though tired and hungry and the food was almost ready, Ezboni got up to go. The host begged him to stay but he would not wait. Soon after he left, his pursuers arrived and found him gone.

Ezboni was a disciplinarian who did not suffer fools easily and furthermore, he had little patience for failure. Given this impulsive character, he would strike at the source of annoyance. When he was the Minister of Communication Transport and Roads in Juba, Ezboni often used to go out inspecting the condition of the roads unannounced. The story is told that one time he slapped the head road worker (*terebeyi*) near 'Buägyi for doing a shoddy job, wherever he stopped to see some work, the workers would make sure that there is more than an arm's length distance between them and Ezboni, in case he got annoyed over some failure and strikes. This could explain why he slapped (if at all) the telephone operator in Khartoum and the Head Scout at Chief Ngere's area.

Ezboni was a principled and incorruptible person. Morris, his close condant for many years, says that Ezboni would not take bribes nor would he offer bribes. In fact, his reputation as one who could not be bribed by Northerners was known to his people, for which they voted for him several times. The Northerners also knew that of him and he would not fall for their flattery. Consequently, nobody dared to bribe him. Ezboni treated public funds with deference and did not use his position to amass wealth and property. So, he died poor. Furthermore, as stated earlier, even when his condition was bad Ezboni did not ask for assistance because in his mind asking for assistance was tantamount to begging.

Ezboni was a courageous person who would speak his mind to anyone, Abel or Nimeiri. In December 1964, when Southerners were being killed in Khartoum, following their riot in the airport, many were frightened and longed to go back to Southern Sudan but they had no money to transporting themselves home to the South. Ezboni, as Minister of Communication and Transport singlehandedly and without Cabinet support gave directives for the week's trains and steamers to take any Southerner wishing to go back to the South to go free of charge. For that, he was roundly criticized in the cabinet and by the newspapers and Northerners in general. He was accused of having done that to fulfill his objective of separation. However, that did not bother him, since in his view that action enabled poor and frightened Southerners to return home. According to him, he had to do that because he saw that the cabinet and the police were doing almost nothing to stop the beating up and killing of Southerners. That free ride by Ezboni made many Southerners who could for years not afford the tickets the chance to go back home and that endeared him to many Southerners.

Ezboni detested the mistreatment of ordinary civilians and always sympathized with the poor, weak and the disadvantaged. Part of Ezboni's problem with Jackson Garaŋwa, the commander of the Kedi'ba Anyanya Group, could be traced to his dislike of the mistreatment of the people that was still being meted out to the civilians by the Kedi'ba Anyanya Group, whereas it had ceased in the areas under the Mayaya Group. Hence, when he heard that Jackson had arrested the elders and chiefs of Kedi'ba, he was incensed and sent a force under Repent Sunday to subdue and bring that Anyanya Group under control.

Ever since he became politically conscious, Ezboni was a Southern nationalist *par excellence*. He strongly believed that the South Sudanese were willy-nilly rail-roaded into a union with Northern Sudanese by the British on no justifiable grounds. He detested the Northern Sudanese mindset and their habit of looking down on Southerners as low class people. He thus had low opinion of those Southern Sudanese who seem to admire, succumb or accept Northern Sudanese superiority. Very early enough he had come to realize that the British had sold the South Sudanese to the Northern Sudanese and so his ambition was how to free them from Northern domination. In his view, that could either be through a strongly federated Sudan or, failing that, a complete separate Southern Sudan.

Ezboni was not a communist, though this label was several times used against him: for organizing a coup against him; excluding from the Second National Convention; and for detaining him.

Because Ezboni was a Southern nationalist he vehemently rejected *kokora* and campaigned widely against it all over the South. He even buried his differences with Abel Alier for the sake of preserving the Addis Ababa Agreement and Southern Sudan, so that it would not be divided. Furthermore, even when his own people frustrated his plans to unite the Anyanya by establishing a GHQ at Lomileŋwa and his colleagues would not allow him to attend the Second National Convention at Angudri and put him under detention on flimsy grounds of being a communist, whereas he was not a communist at all. He never expounded any socialist or communistic ideas nor uttered communistic jargons in his private or public utterances and speeches. He was aware of this false allegation but did not take it against those who created it.

Ezboni was a person who believed in Southern unity. After being forced to abandon the Resistance Movement, he tried to form party/government, the main objective of which was to fight for Southern Sudan national unity and independence but did not have the resources. Just as mentioned elsewhere, he reconciled with Abel during the heat of *kokora* for the sake of the unity of Southern Sudan.

McCall notes that Ezboni was a man of great energy and determination. Without him, ALF would have remained a small east bank organization of no importance. Ezboni gave the ALF a national stature, platform and image that undertook to convince Southerners in different parts of the country that they were fighting for the same cause. Ezboni was the only leader of the Southern Resistance Movement who travelled to many parts of Southern Sudan outside his tribal area, unlike the others (Fr Saturnino, Oduho, Aggrey, Lagu etc) who were mostly confined to their tribal areas. As may be recalled in 1983, he also undertook a similar mission to many parts of the country to convince Southerners that *kokora* was inimical to Southern interests.

Ezboni was a man of ideas, as also stated by McCall. For example, he was responsible for the development of the ALF 'New Policy Program' which included: the separation of the military from civilian administrative matters; dividing the South into manageable regions and appointing governors and district commissioners to run them; integrating and structuring the disparate Anyanya units with a GHQ and Regional Commands; and realizing that arms purchased from the Congolese rebels were totally inadequate for fighting the government army, and therefore arms should be sought from better sources, even China.

It must be mentioned here that those ideas of Ezboni were used by Aggrey Jaden in setting up his administration, when he was elected the President of the Southern Sudan Provisional Government (SSPG) in the Second Convention in Angudri. Those ideas were also later used by the Southern Regional Government for dividing the three Southern Provinces into seven Provinces.

As is known, Southern politics from inception has always been dogged by disagreements between the leaders either because of tribalism and/or rivalry for leadership. For example, there were the William Deng- Joseph Oduho (SANU); William Deng- Aggrey Jaden (SANU); Aggrey Jaden-Joseph Oduho (SALF/ALM); Aggrey Jaden-Gordon Mourtat (SSPG); Abel Alier-Joseph Lagu (HEC); John Garang-Riek Machar (SPLM); and Salva Kiir-Riek Machar (SPLM) of today. It is to be noted that, though he was one of the top leaders of Southern Sudan political establishment, Ezboni was not involved in any quarrel or rivalry with any of the other leaders. From his words, he was only at odds with Abel Alier on a few things. Mainly that Abel was ready to do things so as to end up in the good books of the Northerners, like readily accepting to be imposed by Nimeiri as the President of HEC. He also was at odds with him because of Abel's increasing tribal tendencies. But he quickly mended fences with him for the sake of Southern Sudan. To him, Southern Sudan was bigger than the disagreement with Abel.

His main problem was at home and the reasons for them had been outlined in earlier chapters. Suffice to say at this point that those reasons mainly emanate from the wide chasm between his knowledge and understanding of what is at stake in Southern Sudan and those of the local Anyanya. Despite the indecency, humiliation and outright lie against him that he as a Miza was against the Kädiro, an allegation that was used against him by some local politicians, he did not allow those to detract him from the welfare of the community as a whole. He also did not give any heed to the empty smear campaign during the campaign of 1983 elections in which he was alleged to have been bought by Abel and the Dinka.

Ezboni was a man of the simple people and he enjoyed their company. He did not enjoy opulence and avoided limelight. Yet he was self- condent, resolute and principled. No amount of words or money would dissuade him from his stand, principles and beliefs.

David Bassiouni's View
My View of Ezboni Mondiri Gwonza

In our early days of schooling, and especially in secondary school, we heard about those the first Southerners ever to reach the top of the learning ladder, the university. They were likes of Aggrey Jaden, John Garang (not de Mabior) Louis Buok, Ezboni Mondiri Gwonza, Hilary Logali, Sabino Othow and others. Not all of us met them, but they served as icons and inspirations to us, the generations of Southern students from the single secondary school for Southern Sudan at Rumbek. Out of them, Ezboni was the fourth to be admitted to the University College of Khartoum, behind respectively Aggrey, John Garang and Louis Buok.

I met all of them except John Garang. I met Aggrey Jaden at his home in Atlabara, personally building a *tukl* for his family, after he was dismissed as a Senior Administrator in Malakal, for allegedly declining to raise the Sudan flag on Independence Day. I was touched by his humility and integrity; I met Louis Buok and interacted with him as a senior Administrator in the Regional Government and I met Hilary Logali and despite the difference in age, my wife Mary Nura. Bassiouni and I became very close family friends with him and his wife Erminia Cresensio as I worked on various grass roots political assignments under his dynamic oversight as the Southern Front Secretary-General. I met Ezboni at our home in Juba where, then the South Sudan

General Manager for Shell Oil Company. He used to stop over frequently while carrying out his official functions establishing branches of the Company in the Region.

However, I came to know him more after he formed the Federal Party and when I was a Senior Official in the Regional Government and witnessed his daring go-getter and decisive leadership quality in full play. Thereafter, I knew him more through his involvement in the phases and episodes of Southern political development and vicissitudes in his political career. In the politics of Southern Sudan, I can confidently say that Ezboni Mondiri Gwonza was one of the most prominent South Sudanese political giants and pioneering leaders of the country, who dominated the Southern Sudan political landscape in the period 1956 to 1985, the apex of formative years of the Southern Sudanese Political Movements and Struggle.

It is undisputed that, Ezboni has enjoyed a well-deserved popularity and acclaim among his people for his courage and sacrifices in standing up against the North for the inalienable right of the people of Southern Sudan for federation; and which, in his conviction, should lead to independence. In that conviction, the North singled him out and targeted him for their harshest treatment, including constant harassment and a long imprisonment term for what they believed was the main source of the Southern resistance to their rule. But on the contrary, that treatment earned Ezboni the admiration, respect, and gratitude of the people of Southern Sudan, and which continues unabated to this day.

In politics, Ezboni ascended to this pinnacle of resistance and leadership after making unimaginable sacrifices and self-denial. What set him apart from his contemporaries could be traced to his (varied) character, and which perhaps could be traced to his origin as a son of a policeman. It is said that very early in life, he displayed a strong streak of leadership, fearlessness, independence and leadership. These characteristics, reinforced by the formative environments in which he studied in schools, including Nugent School Loka, Nabumali Secondary School in Uganda, and Khartoum University College, fortified and immensely shaped his spirit of Southern Sudan nationalism; professional and political careers; and personal life. Thus, his inborn passion for fighting against injustice and upholding the rights of the individual and in this case the South Sudanese people, transformed him into the fiery Southern Nationalist he became. Added to that was his formidable physical stature and presence that left no doubt in the minds and eyes of his beholders, wherever he appeared, as a leader in command confident and in control of himself and the environment in which he found himself.

Ezboni was a visionary and an action-oriented person. For example, when he noticed that the Liberal Party was not doing enough to fight for federation he formed his own vehicle, the Federal Party, to achieve the same goal. He also noticed glaring weaknesses in the running of the Southern Resistance Movement (SRM). He thus put forward ideas that would not only reform the Movement but improve its efficiency. Those ideas entailed the following: the historic decision of the Movement to operate from inside the country and not outside; to unify the Anyanya nationally across the three provinces led by one command structure and one general headquarters; to separate civilian affairs from the military by setting up administrative structures; to reduce the size of the provinces to manageable sizes; and so on. For that reason, ALF leadership under President Joseph Oduho appointed him as the Secretary for Defense and tasked him to implement the transformative program. He robustly set out to achieve the program travelling on foot over a large portion of South Sudan. As was the case, those ideas of reducing the size of the three provinces to smaller manageable sizes were used by Aggrey Jaden in the subsequent Southern Sudan Provisional Government (SSPG) as well as by the Southern Regional Government. to divide the Region into seven provinces.[16]

In the Movement, Ezboni also saw the inadequacy of the Catholic Church (then the only source of external support and funds for the SRM) to provide the enough wherewithal for prosecuting the war. He thus broached the idea of getting weapons from China which then was supplying weapons to the liberation movements in Mozambique and Angola.

Ezboni was a person who could forgive and reconcile easily with opponents, especially when it involves the interest of Southern Sudan. For example, despite torture and humiliation and rejection by his own Moru Anyanya, owing to differences and falsehoods levelled against him, he did not forsake them. He instead adopted a Christ-like view of "they did not know/understand what they were doing". Similarly, in the Second Convention in Angudri in July 1967, his colleagues excluded him from participation in the Convention and even imprisoned him on the falsehood that he was a Communist. He had to escape and take exile in Uganda. Despite this treatment, when they needed his knowledge, standing and clout for negotiating with the Government of the Sudan in Addis Ababa, for the sake of

---

16   Eastern Equatoria, Western Equatoria, Lakes, Northern Bahr El Ghazal, Jonglei and Upper Nile. Later Upper Nile was split into Unity and Upper Nile Provinces.

Southern Sudan, he readily accepted to lead the Southern Sudan Liberation Movement (SSLM) delegation to the negotiations. Thirdly, because of his uncompromising belief in indivisible unity of South Sudan, he readily reconciled and worked with Abel Alier in opposition to President Nimeiri's plan to re-divide Southern Sudan and abrogate the Addis Ababa Agreement

Ezboni's valor and sympathy for the suffering underdog could be seen displayed dramatically at the 06 December 1964 Incident in Khartoum when in retaliation Southern Sudanese were viciously being hunted, beaten, or killed by their Northern Sudanese compatriots, blamed for the Khartoum Airport riot.. Ezboni, using his position as the Minister of Transport came out boldly to their aid and arranged extensive transportation to take them home to the South. This in a large part earned him the wrath of the Northerners but it also earned him the admiration, recognition, and reverence of the South Sudanese, as an exceptional leader who could save them at the time of need. They therefore took him as the only leader of substance and courage who could defend and elevate them high in the eyes of the Northerners.

In the post-Addis Ababa Agreement period, Ezboni's hard work was evident in the tarmacking of the main streets of Juba in record time. It was also evident in the laying down the foundations for the rehabilitation of the trunk roads in the country. Furthermore, in the rough and tumble intra-Southern politics, Ezboni stood high above the fray. He vehemently opposed the Re-division (*Kokora*) of South Sudan to the hilt until his demise on September 27th, 1991. Furthermore, he detested corruption and bribery. Never in his engagements in the government did he abuse public trust through misappropriation and/or taking bribe.

Several attributes and contributions of Ezboni could be

listed as follows: like Hilary Logali, Abel Alier and others, he sacrificed his lucrative job in Shell Oil Company in order to join politics to free his people; he formed the Federal Party and for the rst time spelt out what a federal state entails. This frightened the Northerners; for that, he became the first senior Southern Sudanese politician to be jailed for a long spell of time because of the demand for federation; he was solely responsible for transporting frightened Southern Sudanese from hostile Khartoum. That action became one of the reasons for relieving him from the Cabinet and subsequently joining the SRM. On the flip side the very massive number of South Sudanese he evacuated to their homeland boosted the ranks of the Anyanya immensely as a fighting force, endearing Ezboni to them.

In the Movement Ezboni injected new ideas into the work of the SRM both militarily and administratively. And although he suffered rejection by the Moru Anyanya and being sidelined by colleagues, he agreed to lead the SSLM delegation to the Addis Ababa Negotiations. In the post- Addis Ababa period, he rejected *kokora* and campaigned seriously against it, warning the people against its risks to Southern Sudan but to no avail. In the end in 1984, that stand made him lose the elections in his constituency for the first time.

Nevertheless, South Sudan remains indebted to Ezboni Mondiri Gwonza for his dream and fight for federalism and eventual freedom from Northern Sudanese domination. Thus, it is only befitting to accord him recognition, appreciation, and honor for his immeasurable service to the nation and for the sacrifices he willingly and proudly underwent for the sake of his motherland. In view of this, it is right and fair to contend that the outstanding leadership role and contributions which Ezboni made during his struggle for independence, certainly weighed significantly to leading to the freedom and independence we are enjoying today. For that reason, he should be eternally remembered by the people of South Sudan for all his sacrifices and inestimable contributions to the country in their long march to self-determination and independence.

Many people will continue to remember and honor Ezboni for various much appreciated and valued qualities and achievements but, all will agree with me that when that hour came for one Champion to stand up against the North on behalf of his people, the South turned to Ezboni and Ezboni willingly rose up to the occasion with courage and dignity. When he lived, Ezboni served his people and country with limitless love and dedication and sacrifice, upholding the total respect for public probity and the independence, unity and indivisibility of South Sudan.

May his soul rest in eternal peace. Amen and Amen.

Epitaph

Since Ezboni passed away, Southern Sudan has made tremendous progress and several changes have taken place. The most signicant being that, through sweat, blood and tears and facilitated by SPLM/A, South Sudan today is a free and an independent country, the ultimate goal for which Ezboni aspired, struggled and sacrificed to achieve and see. As outlined in the above narrative, it is without doubt that Ezboni has certainly made his contribution towards achieving that goal. For this reason, he must surely be smiling and rejoicing wherever he is with this achievement. But he also would be saddened by what is going on today in the country he fought so hard to achieve.

APPENDIX I: APPROXIMATE MANIFESTO OF THE FEDERAL PARTY

A Paraphrase Abstracted from Dr John Gai Nyuot Yoh's Article

Ezboni and others "decided to form a party which should bear the name of the Southern demand. The architect of the new party was a graduate of Faculty of Arts of the University of Khartoum. The draft USA-type constitution of the Federal Party included among other things":

Federal Constitution in the Sudan, where Southern and Northern Federal States were to form relations on equal grounds.

The constitution of Federal Government should be secular; judicial and executive laws should be regulated and conform to each federal state's legislative laws.

Both English and Arabic should have equal recognition as the two main ofcial languages of Federal Sudan.

Likewise, Christianity and Islam should be recognized as

the two major religions in the country without withstanding the right of individuals who believes in other beliefs or religions (heathenism)

The South should have a separate civil service, in which government employment will be the work of the southern Federal authorities and subject to its laws and constitution

The South should have its education system at all levels; a Southern university was to be instituted, to be regulated by the Southern Federal Government

The immediate return to the South of the three Southern secondary schools: Rumbek, Juba Commercial schools and Maridi Teachers Training Centre

Rapid independent economic development for the South The transfer of the Sudan from the Arab World to African World The creation of independent Southern Army

APPENDIX II:
NEW HORIZON ISSUE
OF 2nd OCTOBER 1991

The Father of Federal System is Dead!

The Founder of the Federal Part in the Sudan and one of the leading architects of the Sudan Ezboni Mondiri Gwonza has died. He passed away on Friday morning September 27 1991, in Khartoum Civil Hospital. After a short illness.

The Chairman of the Revolution Command Council, Lt General Omer Al Bashir, on September 28 issued a statement paying tribute to late Ezboni Mondiri.

In his statement, General Al Bashir described the late as a strong advocate for peace and said late Ezboni laid the basis of the 1972 Peace Agreement and remained committed to peaceful solutions to the problem of South Sudan.

He said that Mondiri was one of the pioneers who laid the basis for the political and national work.

The Revolution Command Council, Deputy Chairman and Head of the High Command for the Implementation of the Federal System in the country, General Al Zubair Mohamed Salih also eulogized late Ezboni.

Late Mondiri comes from Mundri in Western Equatoria. He went to Lui Mission School then to Loka Nugent School, after completing successfully at Loka, late Ezboni was sent to Nabumali High School, Uganda for his secondary education". The paper went on to say that Ezboni joined Faculty of Arts of the then Gordon Memorial College of Khartoum where he became the third Southerner to graduate from the University of Khartoum in early 1950s. After graduation, "he founded and formed the Federal Party in 1957-8 as a result of split in the Liberal Party. He was elected to the Sudanese Parliament but jailed for six years for incitement when he worked to rally support for Federal form of government for the country. After 1964 October, Popular Revolution, he was appointed Minister of Communication in the Transitional Government, the rst Southerner to hold that position.

Late Ezboni however left the country in 1966 [*1965, not 1966*] to work with Southern Opposition groups, where he developed the leadership of the Azania Liberation Front and prominent Commander of Southern forces in Equatoria. *[Ezboni was Secretary for Defence for the whole Southern Sudan and not Commander of forces in Equatoria]*

He was active in Southern Sudan Liberation Movement and played an active role in the negotiations which led to the Addis Ababa Agreement.

Late Ezboni served in the Southern Region High Executive Council. He held several executive positions, including among others, Managing Diretor of Nzara Complex, Melut Sugar Project and others. The Editor- in-Chief of *The New Horizon,* Mr. Mathew Obur, described him as a "Great man and Founder of the Federal Party", adding that he was very active since his time in Rumbek *(not correct Ezboni did not go to Rumbek)*. His friend Mr James *(Tambura)* said "Indeed we have lost a great leader and fighter for freedom".

Until his death Friday, late Ezboni was a member of the High Committee for Implementation of Federal System of rule in the country.

BIBLIOGRAPHY

Abdel Rahim, M. The Development of British Policy in Southern Sudan1899-1947. Middle East

Albino, O. B. The Sudan: A Southern Viewpoint. London: Oxford University Press. 1970

Alier, Abel Southern Sudan. Too Many Agreements Dishonoured. Exeter. Ithaca Press 1990

Beshir, M.O. The Southern Sudan: Background to Conflict. London.

C. Hurst and Company 1968 Collins, R. O. Shadows in the Grass. New Haven, 1983

Douglas, H. J. The Root Causes of Sudan's Civil Wars. Oxford. James Currey Publishers 2003, revised 2011

Douglas, H. J. Twentieth Century Civil Wars. *In* The Sudan Handbook. Edited J. Ryle *et al*. Oxford James Currey Publishers 2011

Fuli, S. Shaping a Free Southern Sudan: Memoirs of our Struggle. Paulines Publications Africa. Kolbe Press Limuru Kenya 2002

Holt, P. M. and Daly M. W. A History of the Sudan Harlow. Longman 2000

Lagu, J. Sudan Odyssey through a State: From Ruin to Hope: MOB Centre for Sudanese Studies, 2006

Logali, H. P. In the Struggle: Autobiography and the Memoirs of Hilary Paul Logali; under press 2023

Magaya, A. M. The Anyanya Movement in South Sudan, Focusing on Western Equatoria 1962-1972. South Sudan National Archives Collection. Printed by Marian Press. Kisubi Uganda 1914

Malwal, B. Sudan and South Sudan: From One to Two. St Anthony Series Publishers. Palgrave Macmillan .U. K. 2015

McCall, S. and Lam A. The Genesis and Struggle of the Anyanya in Southern Sudan. Africa World Books Pty. Ltd 2020

Oduho, J. The Problem of Southern Sudan. Hassel Street Press. ISBN -101014743702; ISBN 13-978-101474301

Ruay, D. D. A. The Politics of Two Sudans, the South and the North. The Scandinavian Institute of African Studies ISBN 91- 7106-344-7 1994

Tingwa, P.O. Lest We Forget: The Root Causes and Defining Events Leading to the August 18 1955 Torit Uprising. paanluelwel.com /2018 / commemoration-63rd-anniversary- of-the-august-18-1955- torit - uprising 2018

Woodward, P. Sudan 1698-1989: The Unstable State. Boulder: Lynne Rienner 1990 and London Lester Crook Academic Publishing. 1990

Yoh, J. G. N. Notes on Foreign Policy Trends in Southern Sudan\ political Military Organization and Parties, (1940s- 1972) A paper presented in Center for African Renaissance Studies. University of South Africa. Pretoria. 2005

INDEX

A
Aba 72, 117, 119-20, 159, 161, 163-4
Abbasia, 205
Abboud, Ibrahim 48-49, 57,56-7
Abdel Bagi 59
Abisai 135
Abugo 116-117
Abu John, Samuel 126, 170
Abur, Emmanuel 129,161,170
Achilles heel 76
Acuil, Dhol 196
Adam 118
Addis Ababa 173, 219
Addis Ababa Agreement 93,110, 172-6, 213, 228
  Abrogation of 189-195,197-201, 220
  Negotiations 207
  Peace talks xvi, 164
Adier, Job 175
Adut, Paul 129
Adwok, Luigi xiv,7, 46, 185
Adyang, Ferdinand 50
Africa 51, 130, 149, 164, 175, 229 230
African xi, xii, 51, 70, 111, 129, 181-2, 224, 230
Africans 17, 51
Ako, Frazer 22
Akol, Lam x, 109
Akoun, Joseph 170
Alam, Dio 7
Alau, Eliaba 34, 43
Albino, Oliver Batali 175
Aliab Dinka 10
Ali Baba, Stephen 73, 76
Alier, Bullen 14
Amadi xi, 10, 39-41, 74, 88, 166

Amarat 206
Amin, Idi1 72
Andago, Aggrey Ndarago 73, 75, 77, 98, 103, 129, 161
Anglican 14
Anglo-Egyptian, Sudan xix, 2, 3 Angola 130, 219
Angotowa 117, 134, 135, 137,
145, 146
Angudri,(military depot) 97, 104, 121, 131-6, 143-6, 150, 167
Angudri Convention 156, 159-162, 165, 213-4, 219
Angunde 75
Anok, Kon 7, 10
Ansar 19
Anyanya ix, x, xi, xvi, 52-6, 66-9, 71-103, 105-6, 108-9, 111-3, 115,
117-134, 137-141, 144-157, 159-
164, 166-8, 170-4, 178-9, 182,
212-5, 218-9, 221, 230
Anyanya Military High Command 126, 170
Anyidi Provisional Government 169, 174
Apaya, William 95
Apollo, Daniel 95
Arab domination 120, 123
  government 104

imperialism 52
World 224
Arabic language 36
Arabic language use 49, 223
Arabism 3
Arabization 6, 24, 49
Arabized ix Arabs 125, 136
Ariendit 7
Atem, Akuot 166
Atlabara 216
August 18 Uprising xiv, 23, 27-8, 45, 72, 230
Avelino,Taban 114
Avokaya tribe 121
Awa Gwonza 10
Awet, Paul 129
Azande Anyanya 126
  politico-military setup 122
  riots xv
Azania Liberation Front (ALF) ix, xi, xvi, 17, 70-1, 105, 226,
Azanian 164

B

Babiker 56
Baggari 144
Bago, Henry 185
Bahr El Ghazal xix, 1, 5,109,112, 118, 120-1, 129, 131, 144, 166,
170, 181-2, 198, 219
Bakhiet, Charles x
Balanda Bviri1 31, 135, 144

Balgo Bindi 134, 160, 169
Bangolo 74-75
Bari 77
Bari tribe 161, 166, 190, 196
Bariŋwa, Yotama 77, 84, 89
Bassiouni, David x, xvi, 209, 216
Bassiouni, Mary Nura 216
Baya, Natania 200
Bentiu 191
Beshir Abbadi 183
Beshir, Darius 21, 30, 32, 43-4, 64 Beshir, El Hag Yousif 74, 77, 82, 100-1, 121
Beshir, Mohamed Omer 229
Bessalia 131
Bily, Musa 30
Biringi,,Francis Wajo 132, 135, 145-6, 196, 202
Biringi, Yosepata 77
Blue Nile Province xix, 51
Bol, Samuel Aru 185, 187
Bombo 164, 174
Bor 71, 186, 188, 190, 192, 204-5 British xii, 2, 4-7, 15, 17-18, 20-4, 110, 181-2, 191, 212, 229
'Bu Diri 90
'Bungit, Bismarck 115
Bungu 168-9
Buok, Louis 14-15, 216
Burri 60
Bussere 14

C
Cairo 25
Cambridge Ordinary Level Examinations 15
Cat out of the bag 194
Catholicism 155
Central Equatoria 119, 121-8, 137- 8, 158, 160, 166-170
Central Equatoria Province 109 Charity Lorna Gwonza 11
Charles Jato Gwonza 10, 77, 80, 83 China 130, 162, 214, 219
Chinese 130
Christian 143
Christianity 46, 121-2, 223
Christmas 50
Christopher Lemeri Gwonza 11 Ciniŋwa, Batwele 77
Cirillo, Peter 97, 108, 129, 161, 163-4
Closed District Ordnance 3
Collins, Robert 229
Congo 9, 55, 62, 72-4, 84, 87, 95-6, 98, 100, 106, 108, 118-121, 129, 131-2,144-6,152,156, 161,163-4
Congolese 78, 96, 214
Conspiracy against ALF 131, 135
Coup,(against Ezboni)131-2, 142, 147
Coup (Abboud) 47, 49

Coup (Omer El Beshir) 205
Cresensio, Erminia Keji 216

D
Dada, David 116-117, 119
Dafalla, Michael, 14
Daŋgoro, Frederick Magot 14, 169-170, 173-5
Darfur xix Darfurians 47
Dawidi, ElIaza 77
Dawidi ,Ngola 91
December 6 riots 59-62
Deims 31, 33, 39, 60
de Mabior, John Garang 204
de Mabior, Enock Mading 174, 178
Deng, Santino 67
Depot 135, 161
Dhol, Camillo 132-133, 143-7 Difficulties with Jack Garaŋwa 100 Difficulties with Repent Sunday 103
Diko 9-10, 75
Dinka 51, 18-9, 133, 139, 161, 164, 186, 189-190, 193-4
Dinkas 139, 188-9
Dito 71, 106, 113, 140
Dodo, Gabriel Pataki 177, 136 Doggale, Paul (Fr) 146
Dumule 173

E
East Africa 149, 164, 175-6
East African 181-2
East Bank 114
East Equatoria Province 109
Eastern Equatoria 52, 106, 112-3, 119, 121, 124-6, 128, 140-1 219
Ed Damer 43, 65, 49-50, 54
Egypt 2, 16, 67
Egyptian 1, 3
Egyptians 2, 4, 7, 18
El Azhari, Ismail 21-23, 25, 34, 36, 45, 64, 73
El Bashir, Omer Ahmed 205, 225 El Khalifa, Sir El Khatim xvi, 5, 23, 57, 63, 71, 111, 208
El Mahdi, Mohamed Ahmed 2
El Mahdi, Saddig 68, 205
El Turabi, Hassan 192, 194, 196, 201
Elemetu, Brown 199-200
Elizabeth Abarayama 11-12
Elizara Gyima Gwonza 11
Emmanuel Ezboni Gwonza 11 English language 3, 35, 46, 223 Equatoria xix, 1, 6, 18, 22-3, 25, 33, 50, 52, 167, 168, 170, 181-2, 186, 189-90, 196
Equatoria Corps 3, 6, 22-3
Equatoria Province Board 18

Equatoria Region 202
Equatoria Regional
Government 205-6
Europe 51
European 9, 15
Europeans 15
Eva Elisa 11
Ezbonis 38

F
Faculty of Arts 15, 223, 226
Fagiri, Abbas 38-40
Faraje 74, 161
Fashoda1 Fertit 21
Florence Ezboni 11
Forestry Department 73
Fuli, Severino xvi, 32, 52, 70, 103, 106, 109, 112-4, 116-8, 120-1,
123-6, 128, 140, 145, 150-1, 153,
157, 163, 168, 229

G
Garaŋwa Jackson (Jeke) x, 53, 73- 4, 76, 78, 82, 84-5, 87, 98, 100,
103, 143, 147, 150, 167, 212
Garang, Joseph Ukel 172
Gbatala, Paul Ali xiv, 24, 33, 42,73- 5, 96, 98, 100, 102, 105, 121-6, 131-5, 142-5,
149, 133, 160
Gbudwe 7

Gbula 116
George 40
Ghorashi 56
Gibia, Watts Roba 79
Gideon, Repent Sunday 73, 75, 77, 98-9, 102-4, 132-6, 143-7, 150-1,
167,173,212
Ginaba, Elisapa 32
Goi, Ferdinand 131-3, 135, 142-7 Gordon Memorial College 15, 18, 226
Gore, Lewis 24
Gori Gye'de 43
Gori Udru 75
Gwonza, Ezboni Mondiri ix, x, xiv, xv, xvi, xvii, 1, 7, 9-21, 26-28, 30-
46, 48-50, 54-5, 57-9, 61-2, 64-7,
69, 71-4, 76, 80-7, 89-90, 93-5, 97-
103, 105-6, 108-129, 131-2, 133-6,
137, 139-157, 159-165, 167, 174-
8, 180-9, 193, 195-9, 201-223, 225-7
Gyikaa, Abarayama 41
Gyirimani, Benedict Tarifo 84-85

H

Hag Yousif 205
Haggar Asalaya Sugar Factory 184
Haggar's Tobacco Company 73
Hassan, Gama 178, 185
Hassan, Romano 14
Hassan, William 97, 108, 129, 134, 136, 139, 161
Haworu, Joseph Oduho xiv, 7, 24, 29, 46, 164, 50-3, 62-3, 70-1, 95, 105-6, 108, 113-4, 117, 119-120, 123, 139-41, 146, 156-7, 159, 164, 176, 178, 184-5, 196, 214-5, 230
Hiteng, Cirino x
Helm, Sir Alexander Knox 23
Hilir, Lotada 24, 33, 39, 42

I

Ibba 121-6, 142, 149, 155
Imatong 24, 108, 165
Imokoru 140
Ingessena 51
Iniŋwa, Francis 'Bädriako 84
Isiro 161
Islam 3, 38, 46, 49, 223
Islamism 3
Islamization 6, 24, 49
Islamized xii
Ismail, Abdin 64
Israel 166, 170, 172
Israelis 171
Italy 131, 144
Iwatoka 73

J

Jada, Simon 117
Jambo, Chief 34, 38
Jambo (Mide) Police Post 87, 89, 94, 101, 103, 145, 149
Jambo, Zakaria Ligyigo 34, 37
Jami Ezboni 11
Jaraba, Yezenaya 13
Jinja 164
Jo'di, Ezboni 34, 73, 103, 145, 151, 161
Jonglei 185, 204, 219
Jose Gwonza 10

K

Kabulu, Joseph 190
Kädiro 10, 74, 101, 102, 150
Kagiko 118-119
Kagyi, Batilimoyo 72
Käjivora, Samuel 24
Kakwa 116, 172
Kamonde, Scopas Juma ix, 72, 106, 108, 132-3, 142, 147, 149, 153, 157-9
Kampala 14, 62-4, 70, 164, 166
Kapoeta 51, 109
Kariŋwa, Stanley 103
Karton 205

Kasiko 91
Kassala 55, 58, 205
Katire 35
Kator 66
Kayanga, Morris Ägyili xv, 21,31-2, 34-36, 43, 54, 72-3, 75-77, 95,98, 101, 103, 129, 132-3, 135, 139, 142-3, 147, 149, 158, 161-3, 211
Kedi'ba 74, 77-8, 84-88, 98-9, 101-3, 150, 212
Kenya x, 229
Kenyi Clan 10
Khalil, Abdalla Bey 47-48
Khartoum xvi, xix, 5-6, 15-6, 18-9, 21, 23, 26-7, 30-3, 35-9, 43-4, 46, 54, 56-68, 86, 111, 113-4, 124, 128, 155, 172, 184, 186, 193-4, 196-7, 202-8, 211, 216, 218, 220-1, 223, 225-6
Khatmiya 16
Kipo 89
Kiir, Salva 32, 215
Kisubi 230
Kitgum 51
Koṛe, Edward 77
Kober Prison 60
Kodi, Ezekiel 185
Kodok 59
Kokora189-200

Kokora decree 200-1
Komoyangi, Äbäbä 41
Komoyangi, Head Scout 128
Kordofan xix
Kosti x, 191
Kuku 115
Kulang, Isaiah 185, 196
Kuze, Eliya xiv, 7, 22
Kwai, Abel Alier xiv, xvi, 29, 172-3, 175, 182,-61, 88-196, 198, 208, 211, 213, 215, 220-1, 229
Kwajena 36
Kyila Ezboni 11
Kyiriri, Samsona 77

L

Lado, Aggrey Jaden xiv, 14-5, 26, 28, 50, 63-4, 70-1, 73, 75, 77, 98, 101, 103, 105, 117, 123, 128, 145, 158-162, 165, 167-9, 176, 214-6, 219
Lainya xi, 20, 88, 183
Lam, Stephen 164
Lanyi 12, 39, 42-3, 80, 88
Lasuba, Tadayo 24
Latuka 71, 106, 114, 140, 146
Lenin Ezboni 11
Libra, Constantine 32

Lodongi, Emidio Taffeng xiv, 24, 52, 75, 96, 113, 122, 124-5, 132, 140, 157,169
Logali, Paul xiii
Logali, Hilary Paul xii, xiv, xvi, 7, 17, 29, 64, 124, 155, 178, 180, 185, 196, 202, 208, 216, 221, 230
Loka 13-14
Loleya, Caesar 14
Loleya Renaldo 24
Lomileŋwa 106, 108, 112, 127-141, 143-7, 151-5 158-9, 164, 210, 213
Lomohidiang 106
London 15, 229-230
Loreze 106, 113, 140
Lorifa 106, 113, 140
Lozo 9-10, 75, 173
Lui1 2, 37, 39-40, 71, 74, 77, 81, 84-6, 89-93, 135, 226
Luŋwa 77
Lunjini 41
Lupe, Elia 14, 46, 72, 95, 159
Lwoki, Benjamin xii, 7, 19, 30

M

Mac, Reuben 186, 189
Machar, Riek 215
Mading de Garang, Enock 174, 178
Maduot, Toby 178
Magaya, Alison Monani 126, 230
Mahdism 3
Mahdist 4
Mahdists 2, 7
Mahgoub, Ahmed 48, 67, 81
Majier, Martin 187
Makerere 14
Malakal 22, 25, 31, 60, 65, 199- 200, 219
Malakia 202
Malanga hill 74
Malish Ezboni 11
Malwal,Bona xvi, 196, 230
Manyang, Samuel 136, 139
Maranyi Ezboni 11
Maranyi Gwonza 10
Maridi 20, 38-43, 73, 88, 90, 100, 106, 108-9, 121-2, 126, 132, 134, 137, 143, 145, 166-7, 224
Mathews, Daniel Kuot 50, 196, 227
Mayaya 75-78, 81, 85-93, 97-103, 121, 212
Mbale 14
Mbale, Alexis 50
Mbäriŋwa, Chief Timon Biro 34, 81, 97
Mboro, Clement 7, 29, 58-60, 73, 117, 185-4
McCall, Storrs x, 72, 99, 109-110, 126, 132-3, 155, 156, 157, 158, 163,168, 213,214
Medeu 10

Mele 75
Melut 184-185, 227
Mide 10, 81, 88-9, 227
Milan 131, 144
Military 47, 49, 52, 55, 87,
99, 109, 112, 126, 149, 170,
174-5, 205
Miri Loko 88-81
Mitika 118
Miza 10, 75, 83, 102, 150,
215
Modi, Anderea 190
Mondisi, Simon 123
Mondu 74
Mongalla 5, 10, 184, 190
Monoja, Luka 197
Monyoro, Clement 73
Mori River 40
Moroŋwa 10
Morta 138, 169
Moru ix, xv, 9-10, 35-7,
41-2, 53,
69, 72-6, 79-84, 86, 94, 96-7,
99-
102, 104-6, 108, 111, 113,
123,
126, 128, 132, 134-5,
139-140,
144-155, 157, 159, 161-3,
166-7,
183, 200, 206, 219, 221
Morus 73
Mosa stream 9-10, 75
Mosques 49

Mourada 61
Mourtat, Gordon xiv, 7, 29,
66, 168, 174, 176, 215
Mozambique 130, 219
Mulla, Elisapana Käbi
103, 127-8, 132, 145, 151,
162-3, 167, 173-4
Mundari 90
Mundri xi, 20, 36, 40, 43,
73-4, 77- 9, 81, 87-92, 94, 99,
101, 103, 108,
149, 163, 173, 181-2, 185,
188,
199-200, 208, 226
Mundukuru 96
Muorwel, Dominic 31
Mursal, Angelo Voga Musa,
Hitler 75
Muslim 121-122, 155
Mutek, Lazarus 113, 139, 141,
146, 157
Mvolo 81

N

Nabumali 14-15, 218, 226
Nairobi x, 168, 175-6
Nanga, Philip 129
Naomi Nagyi 10
National Front 57
National Salvation Army xi
National Salvation
Government 205, 208
National Unionist Party xi,
21, 34, 67

New Policy Program 109-110
dissemination 112-126
Ngamunde, Michael Tawil 41,122, 178
Ngangi, Bullen 24
Ngeṛe Chief 9, 106, 128, 211
Ngiṛi 103, 106, 132, 134, 135-9
Ngor, Zakaria 190
Nhial, William Deng xiv, 7, 29, 51, 62-4, 67-8, 70, 95, 97, 108, 129, 134, 136, 139, 161, 185, 215
Nigeria 67
Nile Provisional Government 168, Nile River xi, xix, 51, 109, 112-5, 118, 120-1, 129, 139-140, 166, 168, 170, 174, 198, 205, 219
NImeiri, Gaafar Mohamed 110, 172, 176-8, 182-4, 187, 191-2, 194-203,211,215
Nimule 55
Northerner 176
Northerners 4-7, 17, 22-5, 28, 30, 33, 36, 43-4, 58, 60-6, 68, 81, 173, 176-7, 180, 184, 190-1, 194, 197-9, 201, 206, 211-2, 215, 220
Nuba 47, 51

Nugent School 13, 218, 226
Nuni 138
Nyakuron 208
Nyambiri 115-117, 126
Nyango Ezboni 10
Nyangwara 108
Nyapea 14
Nyiel, Edward 50
Nyigori,Paul 129
Nyinyizo 32
Nyout, John Gai Yoh 223
Nzara 18, 202-3, 227

O
Obote, Milton 172
Obur, Mathew 50, 227
Ochieng, Pankarazio 50
Odongo,Camillo 132-3, 144, 146-7 Odrande, James 207
Ogyiŋwa 10
Ohure, Saturnino (Fr) xiv, 28, 31, 46, 50, 156, 172
Okaru 14
Olwak Natale 178, 187
Omdurman 39, 60, 205
Othow,Sabino 21
Owen, Deputy Governor 5
Owuru, Isaac 79
Oyet, Nathaniel 50

P
Pajokdit, Alphonse Malek 164 Palotaka 50
Panthou 191

Payam 173
Paysama, Stanislaus xiv, 7
Penkimang 115, 117
Piri Dri 9-10, 41-42, 77, 80
Pojulu 108, 158-9, 183, 200
Pot, Paul 175

R
Rajab, Ismail 36, 77
Ramba, Lubari 185, 198
Rassas, Gismalla Abdalla 29, 199 Rhodesia 5
Rikokawa 74
Ring, Ambrose 187,195-6
Robertson, Sir James 5
Roman Catholic 133
Roro, Faustino 18
Round Table Conference 64-65, 67-71
Rubä, Eliaba Alau 34, 43
Rumbek 20,32,50,85,136,192, 216, 224, 227
Rume, Marko xiv,22, 31, 50,72, 95,115, 117, 120
Russie, Johnx, 72, 84,147

S
Sadaraka, Abisai 135
Sara Ezboni 11
Secretariat (ALF) 106, 114, 140 Selassie, Emperor Haile 176, 181
Sennar 184

Seyi, Gwonza 10
Shaggara 60
Shambat 60
Sharia 182, 194, 201-2
Shukole 115
Singo 9-10, 77, 79, 81
Small, Kenneth 98
Southerner 21, 61, 176, 211, 226 Southerners 3-6, 14, 18-9, 21-2, 24-6, 28, 30, 38, 44, 46-7, 49-50, 57-63, 71, 81, 97, 120, 143, 159,
162, 172, 174-6, 180, 185, 189-
191, 193-5, 197-8, 201-2, 211-2,
214, 216,
Southern Front 57, 58-9, 63-68, 188
Southern Regional Government xvi, 177, 180-1, 189, 191-2, 194, 200-1
Southern Sudan Provisional Government 159-160, 162-3, 165, 167, 219
Stigand, Chauncy 10
Sudan African Closed District Union (SACDNU) 50, 54
Sudan African Liberation Front (SALF) 70-71
Sudan African National

Union (SANU) 50, 54-5, 62-4, 67-8, 70, 72, 185
Sudanization 19-21
Sudan Peoples' Liberation Army (SPLA) xii
Sudan Peoples' Liberation Movement (SPLM) xii, 204
Sule, Abdel Rahman xiv, 7
Sundays 50
Surur, Eliaba James 119, 159, 169, 183, 197, 200
Swaka, Serafino Wani 266, 182
Sworo, Gordon 127

T
Tadayo 24
Tambura 122, 131
Tambura, Joseph James 29, 181, 196, 199-203
Tanda Louis 202-203
Tanzania 67
Telephone exchange incident 64-65
Tere, Benjamin 73, 75-6
Tier, Paul 200
Tiga, Yorama Lalume 85
Tingwa, Alice ix
Tingwa, Obodaya 37, 41
Tingwa, Peter (Prof) ix, x, xv, xiv, xvi, 97, 108, 129, 161, 163-4, 187, 230
Tongun, Daniel Jumi xiv, 22, 64, 95, 117-120, 127, 187, 159
Tongun, John 50
Tonj 51
Tore River 136
Tore Wande 77, 135-6
Torit xiv, 6, 20, 22-5, 46, 72, 109, 122, 122, 230
Toto, Eliaba Ginaba 14, 34, 43
Tul 106, 108-9, 111, 145, 165
Turco-Egyptian 1, 3

U
Ucini, Filberto 131, 144
Uganda xvi, 14-7, 51, 53-4, 62, 67, 71, 95-6, 106, 108-9, 141, 146, 159, 163-4, 168, 172, 174, 186, 218-9, 226
Ugandan 15, 140, 156
Ugandans 15
Ukel, Joseph Garang 172
Umma Party 28, 45, 48, 67
Unionist 198
Unionists 196, 199, 201
Unity Party 67
Unity Province 191, 219
University of Khartoum 223, 226 Upper Nile xix, 1, 109, 112, 118, 120, 129, 170, 193
Urugi 114

V
Verona Fathers 132, 135
Vice 168, 178, 186, 197

W
Wad Medani 32
Wandi 77
Wani, Clement 117
Warajwok 71
Warille, Benjamin 200
Warille, Noel 43
Wata, Michael 14, 24
Wau 5, 20, 25, 56, 61, 65, 71, 131, 144, 182, 199-200
Wel, Yithak 190
Wiew, Andrew 185
Western Equatoria 101, 119, 121- 8, 166-170, 219, 226, 230
Western Equatoria Province 109
Wil, Franco Garang 46
Wol, Ambrose 58
Wol 174, 178, 185, 201
Wyld, Major 5, 18, 22

Y
Yambio 5, 8, 22, 109, 121-125, 166
Yanga, Joseph Lagu xiv, xvi, 7, 29, 52-5, 72,74,76,96,101,105,109, 113,120,122,126,140-1,160, 164, 167-172, 174, 178, 185-7, 189-190, 193-4, 196-8, 214-5, 230
Yanni 40
Yei 20, 40, 43, 75, 77, 88, 90, 92, 102, 106, 109, 128, 136, 145, 161, 166, 181-2
Yeri 81
Yirol xi
Yona, Philip 197
Yondoru 158, 183
Yugusuk, Zakaria Wani 14, 30, 34

Z
Zaire 109, 117-8
Zalingei 59
Zande 121, 166, 171, 202-3

www.ingramcontent.com/pod-product-compliance
Lightning Source LLC
Chambersburg PA
CBHW011147290426

44109CB00023B/2521